POETRY WALES

poetrywales.co.uk

Editor Zoë Brigley
Reviews Editor George Sandifer-Smith

EDITORIAL

The theme of remembering has accumulated in this issue, beginning with the intention to honour the centenary of one of Wales's most important poets, Dannie Abse. I met Dannie Abse when I was about ten years old, and my mother took me to a launch of *A Young Man from Cardiff* (published by Seren in 1991). I was very taken by this generous writer with such a keen sense of humour and fun. After the reading, he was extremely kind, recommending that I read *Ash on A Young Man's Sleeve* (1954), which I did. It's intriguing now to read the tributes here, written by people who knew him well, speaking about the impact he had and continues to have on the writing community. It was also a pleasure to hold a conversation with Lynne Hjelmgaard and Penelope Shuttle; both talked about the balance in creative partnerships – Hjelmgaard and Abse, Shuttle and Redgrove – but perhaps most importantly about their own poetic genius as individuals.

Our poetry community has been taking time to absorb the loss of the brilliant poet Gboyega Odubanjo, who died suddenly at the end of August 2023, and who I worked with at *Magma Poetry*. Thanks go to the Poetry Business who allowed us to reprint 'There is Joy Breaking Here' from Odubanjo's *Aunty Uncle Poems* (2021), a poem that celebrates ordinary joy in the face of small and large difficulties. The poem plays on the double meaning of 'breaking' which could be the breaking of light, or the breaking of the spirit. The aunties and uncles, however, persevere. Odubanjo's family and friends set up a fundraiser for a Gboyega Odubanjo Foundation for low-income black writers which we would encourage readers to donate to if you can. (See <https://linktr.ee/poetrywales>).

Memory, grief, and loss have wound themselves through this issue from Nurain Ọládèjì's 'Picking Up a Stray Grief' to Paul Henry's elegy to a lost sister, 'Like the Sea', and a duo of poems by Virgil Suárez and Jo Mazelis that delve into memory. Other than that, there are great poems from everywhere, like translations of Fabio Morábito (based in Mexico City) by Richard Gwyn; a compendium of very short poems; and winners from the Wales Poetry Award. Back in issue 57.1, Kris Paul wrote an article on Welsh experimental writing, a theme important to us at *Poetry Wales*. An article by Christodoulos Makris follows up on innovative poetry, with an article on the avant-garde in Ireland, which could provide food for comparisons regarding what has happened and is happening in Wales.

We also introduce Tangie Mitchell, an alumnus of the Obsidian Foundation, who will be contributing editor in spring 2024 along with Welsh poet Taylor Edmonds; Mitchell provides here a workshop on nightlife, love and (be)longing. Welcome to Mitchell, to Edmonds, and the other contributing editors joining us in 2024 in partnership with the Obsidian Foundation, including Des Mannay, Fahad Al-Amoudi, Kandace Siobhan Walker, and Zakia Carpenter-Hall.

ZOË BRIGLEY

GBOYEGA ODUBANJO

There Is Joy Breaking Here

and uncle is drunk already. uncle has his nephews
his special brew holding him up and happier
than the rest of us this bloodshot day of meat
and gisting. uncle grills burgers in knock-off birkenstocks.
plays coquet for aunty long since tired of his face
and fatuous self. uncle deep in meniscus. uncle cracks
the bone and swallows marrow. does not sweat or spill
a sip. Uncle of independent means. clapping on the ones
and threes. jiving. got the old lady and the home office
and type 2 diabetes and maze and frankie beverly
                                        clapping him on

NURAIN ỌLÁDÈJÌ

Picking Up a Stray Grief

> *"When I'm crying, if stream flows, leave me alone.*
> *When I'm crying, if rain falls, leave me alone." –* Aṣa

The taxi stopped at a bakery, and the old woman who
flagged us down lifted her basket of freshly bought
bread into the trunk and came around
to sit on the passenger seat.

We had barely settled back on the road when she
started to cry; her head dropped to her chest and
she pulled the hem of her wrapper up to dry her eyes.

She cried quietly, privately, and the driver could only
say "Don't cry anymore, mama," because what else
could he say to a woman old enough to be his mother
and my grandmother? I wanted to ask why she cried
but I knew better than to disrupt such an intimate event.

Her clothes were old but clean; her face wrinkled
yet gracefully. Her wares in the trunk, which I could
see her selling at a small stall, were roughly
the cost of one leg of my shoes, and remembering
my friend being impressed by how cheap
I got them, I looked away from my feet.

She alighted, thanked the driver, and lifted her wares
to the curb. As we pulled away, I did not turn
to glance at her. Her grief, dangling like a pendant,
had just swung to rest on the left side of my chest.

PAUL HENRY

Like the Sea
i.m. Julia Bentham

Penny, this town was almost ours.
Your mother's double at eighteen
you slide back in on the same track
that set her free.

                What's forty years
to a railway platform, a promenade
where the tide's small change rolls in
and out?

        We wave at the same moment,
the same brown eyes and station clock.
Her old guitar is strapped to your back.

Is it my boyhood self makes you turn
as you pass the castle, unsure
if the line ends here

              or here
beneath the pier's slot-machine?

Conspiracies of light confuse the time,
the glazed faces staring out to sea,
the *Sunshine Home for Blind Babies*,
the empty paddling pool ...

               Penny
this town was almost ours.

               Its tide
down Penglais Hill's slipway
draws our first and last breath.

       ★

Walk with me now, up Maeshendre
home off the bus from Comins Coch,
not by my side

           but five steps ahead,
five years, as my older sister.

Dilys and Dandy snap at our heels.
Mary Coffee waves from her porch.
It's bacon and eggs and fried bread
at number 18.

         Our mother whispers
because her ghost is singing tonight
in the washed away King's Hall.

      ★

If we crouch on the dark shingle
Penny we might hear her still

where the waves lick the bandstand
and shrug off their gowns.
If we dip our hands

         and sift
these ruins of her concert hall
in on the tide

        we might hear
her songs of cynefin.

         And if we sing
(Penny, these new strings
will settle)

        if we sing
we might hear her still, the sea
singing through us.

st. 16: *cynefin*: (Welsh; pr. 'kuh-neh-vin'). No literal translation exists. *'Rootedness'* or *'the place of your multiple belongings'* come close.

JANE BURN

When Pauline Sings *Big River*

"If you believe that there's a bond
  Between our future
  And our past
  Try to hold on to what we had"
               – From *Big River*, by Jimmy Nail

Have you ever watched somebody stand up and sing   no music, no strings
or symphony   stand up and sing   a little worse for wear, maybe for drink
and tune themselves back to the past   Pauline sings Big River   and
every line says   *gone   it's all gone   there is absolutely nothing left*

We all need a tune to hang our tears upon   I see that my friends are old
that death is feeling its way   into their flesh   they are returning
in their thoughts   to some old street   some old face   every line says

Remake the place you were happiest   oh, nostalgia   the cursed rose
that settles its tint upon the brain like bliss   like time's narcotic twin   *Big
River*   Remember   the people crying here were children   once upon a

Tyne   I saw a heron set its skinny legs   into your travelling length
build itself into a perfect embodiment of pain   I saw it   clutching
the rock like a fist clings to rage   such a long way you have come,
river   North and South to Watersmeet   then out toward the sea

JANE ZWART

Small Craft

To trust yourself to what might easily be
buffeted. To feel every swell, to know oceans
ride roughshod over dinghies' rudders.

To fold yourself to fit a soapbox cockpit.
To kiss your knees, to brave the hill where
steering is the runner-up to homing gravity.

To barrel the tiny plane down a dark stripe,
to lift, pinwheels spinning, in a howdah
thunder could buck from clouds' grey backs.

To live. To strap children into car seats,
to appoint the body the heart's deputy, to turn
a single corner, to love any little thing.

SADDIQ DZUKOGI

A Good Muslim

Last night, in a basement, I was with a bunch of kids
I met on the rugby team. The stereo in the corner
showed us the back of its throat, while the walls palpitated
anxiously to the sound of hip-hop. White bodies given in
to black music. I only started listening to Pac and Biggie
lately. Do you know this song? *No*, I replied. Do you smoke?
No. It was a party I mistook for practice
but everything, even grief, can be turned into a sport.
I picked up a Ping-Pong ball and aimed it into cups,
half-filled with beer, stacked close to each other
like makeshift cathedrals of debauchery
I wondered if they judged me for not drinking.
Are you a good Muslim? One of the boys
asked while the girl beside him winked at me, her
brow-hair well darkened with eye-pencil. At nights,
when I open the Quran and read, yes, I am
a good Muslim then, because I see the grey face
of God take form on a page, a universe, and each word
cleanses me of desires that will be rekindled like dawn
when morning comes upon my beautiful bones.

JOSE HERNANDEZ DIAZ

Blue Lobster Soliloquy

1 in 5,000 north Atlantic lobsters are born bright blue. Sometimes, I wish I was born bright blue. But then, no, I can't decide. To be famous, infamous or just blend in with the crowd? Which is better? Aren't we all essentially the same, anyway? Who decides all of these random circumstances we are born into? No one? God? Mary? The lambs? No one, right? Random occurrence, right? That's where we're at in history, I'm assuming. Anyway, a bright blue lobster, how romantic. Poetic. Normal. Iconoclastic. Mundane. Obscure. Either way, I'm hungry, where's that peculiar lobster?

BETHANY HANDLEY

Hiya Butt Bay

Castors to the sky, face to the sea
I'm sitting on my back wheels, leaning against my friend
on Rest Bay beach as we sink into the wet sand

her weight willing us closer to the waves, driving
us forwards like she's back in a scrum, gripping my handles,
her feet digging as I clasp my push rims.

We wheel over a sandcastle, sinking into its moat,
the turret's flag flying from my spokes,
crushed walls in my tread. Dog walkers and families

stare as we giggle, my wheels
submerged to the axel. A man approaches us,
clears his throat, informs my friend that when he

takes his mother-in-law out
he finds its best to drag her backwards.
I give him my *piss off mate, we're doing fine thanks* look

but we try it anyway, slowly turning
our backs to the sea,
admire our tyre marks stretching their limbs

see the children pretending to be a train
as they jog down our tracks and we're pushing
quicker towards the water, sand surrendering.

I used to seek footprints that obscured
my own, moved within another's trace.
Now I survey my trenches with delight

(you could read them from a drone)

you wouldn't guess they're footprints:
two unsteady lines claiming the land.

KAREN GOODWIN

Grapefruit

The midwife lowers you in the silver dish of her scales,
weighs a June harvest
a windfall, seven pounds!

Precious haul, I nurse you on my lap –
some mothers keep score of which breast
was last emptied with a ribbon tied to their wrist –

I decide on a hairband, right hand, right breast
While you decant air from me, blood, flight
She draws me a grapefruit on a napkin

Cut across its navel to demonstrate
How each fleshy segment fills with milk
immediately after a feed

And if not emptied entirely
Are prone to blister like bladderwrack.
My mamgu was an excellent cook

Made grapefruit in creme de menthe
For visiting relatives, it was her special dish
Requiring a staunch stomach. I could never manage it.

The viscous liquid in my breast
goes sour, pumped into clear glass bottles
And stowed in the fridge, blue tinged in weeks.

Doctor and Magician

Extracts from a tribute to DANNIE ABSE in what would have been his one hundredth year curated by TONY CURTIS

Read the complete online pamphlet with the full tributes which these extracts are taken from at www.poetrywales.co.uk/doctor-and-magician/.

Introduction by TONY CURTIS

I am so pleased to be able to bring together this tribute to Dannie Abse, one of our most significant poets. In common with several other poets of my generation and that which followed, I owed so much to Dannie's generous time, wisdom and the practical support of "Our man in London."

Most contributors knew Dannie well: Jeremy Robson was a friend and publisher of the poet for over forty years; Cary Archard started Poetry Wales Press, which became Seren Books, and was indebted to Dannie and Joan's generous support at Green Hollows, their house in Ogmore by Sea; Lynne Hjelmgaard was Dannie's partner in his final years. Both Owen Sheers and I were privileged to have Dannie as a mentor and friend in our personal and writing lives.

My first encounter with Dannie was as a member of the audience at Swansea University (U.C.W. Swansea) in 1967 where I was reading English. Here was a (youngish) man who was handsome, Welsh, famous and who read accessible poems with distinctive voices and themes. Dannie Abse's poem 'In the Theatre' left us stunned. Its use of voices and direct speech harked back to my encounters with Robert Frost, Eliot and Robert Browning, and affected me as powerfully as the latter's 'My Last Duchess'. What I had learned from Frost and Browning and what was confirmed by Dannie's writing and performance was the freedom of writing a recollection through the experiences and voices of others. "He do the police in different voices" – Dickens and T.S. Eliot. What was exceptionally powerful was Dannie's reading of that poem for an audience. The voices and his voices were dramatic, gripping and shocking. Few contemporary poets have achieved the power of story-telling and the music of poetry in a single text as often as in Dannie's poems. He spoke of himself as wearing the white coat and the purple cloak – both doctor and magician, the man of cold, professional detachment always pulled towards the life of the imagination and the healing of art.

An extract from Dannie Remembered, a Personal Memoir by JEREMY ROBSON

Erudite, compassionate, socially relevant, entertaining, Dannie's poetry was quite different from that of any of his contemporaries, both in its range, philosophical depth, and strong narrative quality, his vocabulary wide and precise. As Dannie put it, 'there are many words, but in a poem only one right one'. Whether it was his Welshness, his Jewishness, or the medical experiences he drew on which most strongly fired his strong poetic voice is hard to say, for all were vital ingredients though not the only ones.

Unlike his brother Leo, the political firebrand, there was little trace of a Welsh accent when he spoke, perhaps because he studied and worked most of his life in London, but when he read his poems aloud his voice was uniquely lyrical. His links to Wales remained strong and while his parents were alive, he returned to Cardiff frequently. Later, when his medical life became less demanding, he and Joan bought a house in Ogmore-By-Sea where they spent a good deal of time. It clearly reminded him of his childhood, and it is perhaps no coincidence that Welsh subjects started to enter the vocabulary of his poetry. I was glad, when I started my own publishing company, to be able to reissue Dannie's early autobiographical novel, *Ash on a Young Man's Sleeve*, now a classic in which with humour and tenderness he recalled growing up in Wales in the 1930's with his brother Leo, and his eldest brother Wilfred who was to become an eminent professor of psychiatry, both of whom influenced him greatly. Dannie was a superb anecdotalist with a wide repertoire of entertaining stories, as his various volumes of autobiography confirm. He was particularly close to his mother, and loved to recall that when his first book of poems came out, she strolled into Lear's bookshop in Cardiff and asked for a copy. 'I'm afraid we don't have it in at present,' she was told. 'However, we do have Dylan Thomas's new book.' 'But,' responded his mother indignantly as she marched haughtily out of the shop,' my son is the Welsh Dylan Thomas.'

With regard to Dannie's Judaism and its influence on his poems, I should add here, as anyone who knows his poem 'Odd' will appreciate, he was not in any way an observant Jew, though a proud one and the weight of recent Jewish history weighed heavily on him. As he famously remarked, 'Hitler made me more of a Jew than Moses did.' His feelings were later enhanced, I'm sure, by our reading tour of Israel, where history stares you in the eye at every turn, and he was clearly both moved and gratified by the response his poems evoked in the six readings we gave there. Back in London I remember him telling me, laughing as he did so, about some Orthodox rabbis knocking on his door looking for a charitable donation and going on to chide him for not belonging to a synagogue. Finally, exasperated and as a last sally they said, 'If you don't belong to a synagogue, you won't be able to have a proper burial'. To which Dannie replied, the door half closed, 'I'm not going to die!' If only that had been so.

An *extract from* Watching Football by CARY ARCHARD

In the garden, outside the main Cardiff City stadium, there is a tree planted in the memory of Dannie Abse, one of the Bluebirds' most devoted supporters. As he explained later, 'I was nine years of age when I went to Ninian Park for the first time on my own. I watched a game between Cardiff City and Torquay United'. It was 1933 and the crowd handed the young boy all the way down to the front right behind the goal posts while the band played; 'There, breathing in neighbouring pipe and Woodbine or Craven A cigarette smoke I could observe, at acrid eye-level, my blue-shirted heroes display their rare skills and common blunders'. These early memories went deep. In his 80s, he still travelled from his Golders Green home to his house in Wales on the weekends when Cardiff City were playing at home. He'd leave Ogmore-By- Sea straight after lunch, often in a blue shirt and his favourite old overcoat that had seen many matches, to get to the ground in time for the 3 O'clock kick off.

The tree is one memorial to his devotion to the Bluebirds, his poem 'The Game' written in his early thirties (from in his collection *Tenants of the House: Poems 1951-1956*) another; it is probably his best-known poem. It captures the excitement and disappointments of the young supporter but from an older and wider viewpoint. It's that 'wider' viewpoint that is striking about 'The Game'. The poem may be about Cardiff City, but it is also a very European, indeed cosmopolitan poem in its range of allusions cultural and political. The collection in which it appears is very carefully organised into five sections. This poem appears in the first, 'Metaphysical Ironies', and these are poems which are often quite dark, allegorical in form, fond of paradox. The first poem in the section, 'The Master', suggests the metaphysical nature of what is to come and even the mystical roots of poetry; 'I move my mouth but Your new words I shout'. It's as though the poem is being used to explore another, emerging level. And the speaker in 'The Game' moves beyond obvious descriptions of the game to wider, deeper concerns.

'The Game' is a poem which shows that a game can be a microcosm for larger events, that emotions in a game are not unrelated to emotions in the political sphere. It connects to the debate about how you cannot separate sport from politics. It shouldn't be forgotten too that this poem has special relevance to the time it was written, in the 50s. Dannie Abse felt that poetry written by the new "Tenants of the House", the Movement poets, was dangerously insular and narrow. As he characterises them: [they] 'dare not whistle in the dark again. / In bowler hats they sing with sharp, flat voices/ but no one dances, nobody rejoices.' 'The Game' in contrast, is full of sounds and music, from the 'Hoompa' of 'the brassy band' to the 'shout' at the end; and in between there's even 'a distant whistle' to be heard, one that could be coming out from the dark. In the book's last poem, the poet offers us what he hopes is the opposite of 'flat voices': 'To those with cold hands I offer fires / and sing the catastrophes.'

An extract from A Visit to Dannie by OWEN SHEERS

I can't remember exactly why I was visiting Dannie that day, most likely to go for lunch in his favourite cafe on the Finchley Road, or to take a walk in Golders Hill Park, but whatever the occasion, I was early. Too early, as it turns out. Having pressed the doorbell of his home I waited on the doorstep. I was used to Dannie answering his door quickly, the blurred shape of him approaching through its decorated glass – a distinctive penumbra of unruly grey hair, that particular impish tilt of his head above sloping, eager shoulders. His disarming smile. But on that day no out-of-focus Dannie appeared. There was just silence. I looked down at the doorstep and saw two milk bottles, full, uncollected. Should I be worried?

I rang the bell again, holding my breath and listened hard to the empty hallway on the other side of the door. Oh no. This was a year or so after the death of Dannie's wife, Joan. He'd somehow ridden that sudden and eviscerating grief with grace and fortitude (partly kept afloat, as we'd all find out later, by writing a regular diary of loss and love). He was fit, well. But he was also in his mid-80s...

But then there he was - that impressionistic version of him emerging into the hallway through the glass. I breathed out. Or was that front door in fact solid? Was there no glass? Maybe. Am I just imagining this memory of seeing Dannie come into focus as he approached because it's a convenient metaphor... perhaps. But if I am, somehow, I think Dannie would have liked that - painting the facts with a storyteller's brush – so I'll keep it in. I learnt the word 'ludic' from Dannie, and I think of him every time I hear it or say it. So yes, in the spirit of the ludicity that informed so much of Dannie's writing and conversation, I'll stick with this picture of his indistinct self, growing through the decorated glass, then coming into sudden clarity as he opened the door.

Clarity, yes. But not wearing the expression I was expecting. There was Dannie, in all his Dannie-ness, but without that disarming smile, composed as much of wisdom as of play. No, in its place was... a frown. A distant look in his eye. Maybe, even... irritation?

'Oh', he said. 'You're early.'

I looked at my watch. It was ten past ten. I actually thought I was late. 'Didn't we say ten?' I asked

'No,' he answered. 'Eleven. We said eleven.'

'Oh. Shall I...?'

'No. No, come in,' he said, as he walked back into the hallway. 'You might be able to help me actually.'

And so I walked in, closing the front door behind me. When I turned round the hallway was empty again.

'In here!'

His voice had come from an open door off the hallway. I followed it and found myself, for the first time, standing in his study.

When I entered his study, I found Dannie standing in front of his desk which in turn was placed in front of a large bay window looking out onto the street. He was staring up at this window where a single bee was vibrating across the glass, trying to find the air it could see but no longer feel.

'I was working on a poem,' he said. 'A line, but then this bee got in. I've been trying to let it out.'

And then it all made sense. A quiet morning, some time to fine-tune a poem, discover the right cadence of a line. The poet's solitary pursuit of experience in the shape of words. And then a bee, disturbing that pursuit. And then, after the bee, me, an hour too early. A double interruption. No wonder Dannie had met me with a frown.

He pointed up at the higher glass where the smaller frames at the top could be opened.

'If you get up on the desk,' he said. 'Do you think you could reach that window and open it?'

I probably made some kind of a joke about this not being the job for two short Welshmen, but did what Dannie had suggested, stepping carefully first onto his desk chair, and then even more carefully up on to the desk itself. When I looked down at my shoes, which felt suddenly too-large, clumsy, I saw between them the sheet of A4 Dannie had been writing on. And there was the line, or rather the lines. A neat, handwritten copy of a poem leading to a series of crossed out sentences, alternative words suspended over others, false starts and almost endings. The coalface of Dannie's life with language.

It turns out I could reach the window, and having opened it the bee soon found it's air and flew out into the London morning. Like a poet finding their line, perhaps. I got down off the desk, and when I had found the Dannie I knew to be back. There was the smile again – reassuring, curious. Kind.

'Coffee?' he said.

An extract from Listening to Dannie by LYNNE HJELMGAARD

Listening to Dannie for the first time at the Torbay Poetry Festival was like hearing a familiar voice, one that I knew yet had never encountered before. I'd never heard of Dannie Abse. I was living in Copenhagen at the time, though would visit my children in Wales.

When I think back to the day I travelled to the Festival, I was still undecided about whether to attend. I even boarded the train bound for Torbay telling myself I could always get off the train. *Get off, go back to Denmark*, a voice was telling me as I gazed at my return ticket.

But I stayed on the train, not knowing I would meet Dannie there. Not knowing that after I had heard him read from *The Presence* at the evening meal on Saturday night, and asked him to sign his book, that this would change my life.

He told me later that he had looked for me at breakfast the next day, waiting to see if I would show up. I told him that I had seen the back of his head at the breakfast table (he was sitting alone) and contemplated for a few moments whether to join him but decided to have breakfast in the adjoining room.

That afternoon I was driven to Torbay Station by a friend. Dannie, by chance, was seated at the bottom of the stairs waiting for his train. We decided to get on the same train back to London. On the way Dannie showed me his notebook filled with various drafts of his poems and asked to see mine. My notebook was luckily buried in my suitcase beneath other suitcases in the corridor. At the time I didn't think I was ready to show him any poems.

When I'd had a chance to read *The Presence*, and some of Dannie's other books, I noticed that we not only wrote about bereavement, (we were both recently widowed) but we had a similar sensitivity and appreciation for nature and for places where we had lived. He wrote about the people closest to him – love poems to his wife Joan and poems about his children, other family members, and poets and artists he admired. And of course, there were poems from his experiences as a medical doctor. He paid attention to small everyday moments, found beauty in the ordinary.

As Dannie wrote in his Author's Note to his *Collected Poems* 'I realise how much they are rooted in and from my life experiences, some mundane, some dramatic. I recall words of Rilke whom I read when I was a young medical student, 'In order to write a single verse one must be able to return in thought to unexpected encounters, to days of childhood that are still indistinct, to nights of love... But one must also have been beside the dying, must have sat beside the dead in a room with open windows and fitful noises.'

Shortly after he died, I walked to his house with such a fever, to hold some of his favourite books again, spend time in his study, inhale his library, relive that feeling of belonging and sense of home that Dannie gave me.

And in my pocket, I still had his favourite pen that I used to borrow. I wrote a poem as a result of these walks back and forth to his house: *Your Pen Rushes to My Hand* (*A Boat Called Annalise*, Seren, 2016).

I recently found this note about Dannie that I wrote shortly after he died in 2014. We had been together for six years.

We had six borrowed Christmases

Even your house confides
to the apple tree like a lost friend.
And your two favourite magnolias
crying: let me in.

During my walks through the Heath
I hear you in the silence: *Green Green
I love you Green*, as I held an envelope
in my pocket addressed to us both.

No more evening phone calls
or morning visits to the café,
trysts on weekends or
reciting poetry in the dark.

Whenever we travelled together, he would always place his slippers beside the bed, and his clock on the side table. I had no need for slippers or a clock. Where was time with so much brightness?

TONY CURTIS

Ida John in Paris, 1907

That morning in the maison de santé after the storm,
when the nuns had finished their prayers and left them to it,
Augustus and Ida toasted each other with glasses of Vichy water,
her coverlet still strewn with fresh violets.
Then she slept, with small movements and mutterings of dreams,
before, that afternoon, passing away in her sleep,

Augustus, with a strange wide-eyed elation, ran away
and drank himself through the next three days,
missing her funeral and the baby's first nights.
He was beyond it all, alone, and did not know who he was.

Henry Lamb and Ambrose McEvoy saw to the business,
a short service and the cremation at Père Lachaise.

When the workman drew her out of the cooling retort,
what was left of Ida was the white spectral form of her body
which they both recognised as her –
the skull, limbs, the cage in which the baby had grown.

Then he struck the slab with a crowbar
and the skeleton crumbled to dust,
each speck of her held in the air
for what seemed like an eternity.

STEPHANIE POWELL

Night worker, questionnaire

How is the quality of your sleep?

How much of the day do you
spend in bed?

Does the tidal stickiness of the city keep
you awake? (y/n)

Or roadworks restrain you
by headlock? (y/n)

What can you translate from the stir and fall of
voices in the room next door?

Do you wake-dream
limb on limb
bedsheets in star-jump ripples? (y/n)

Have you lost your sex-drive? (y/n)

Lately, have all your fish died of
inattention? (y/n, discuss)

Additional comments:
The body fights the upturned day
it won't bend to being awake all night
living between the walls

you are unsewn
           your guts are going to shit

At your back the tourist harbour, the clear quiet air and
mosquito net of stars, you move stealthier
eyes cast long over Blackwattle Bay, the lights
go out one by one in Balmain, car keys dagger sleepily
in one hand

PENELOPE SHUTTLE

cockcrow

how early
is the morning
with its wand of tears?

is the morning early
when the seafront bus snuffles by?

how early
is the morning
this far from home?

is the morning early
if the halfmoon's still there

and
how are you
spelling *early morning*?

LYDIA HARRIS

hasyl nott

and the space was covered in ice
and the space was a slow forest
no bigger than a thimble
round, brown, hard-shelled

it fell from its husk
after seven months growing
it wasn't chert or quartz
or pitchstone or pumice

no more than a small shadow
a toe-bone found in a midden
a tomb for the living
small heart, crouched in a case

CATH DRAKE

The Manager

The floor is riddled with traps, set to react to my feet.
I have acquired a walking stick to test the safety
of each carpet square before I place a foot down.
A trap can take a foot whole, drain blood and it's not easy
to release. When I call for help, I get instructions
on how to use the photocopier/scanner or I'm given
the corporate strategy. The Manager doesn't even point me
toward the flimsy plasters in the first aid cabinet.
She has also installed auto-collapse in my chair so I must
assemble heavy steelwork each morning to force it to hold.
My computer fires hot embers when I hit the x or t key.
I must use alternative words when writing reports or emails –
the x often catches me out. If I've not been mindful,
if I'm recovering from wounds, burns, bruises, blindness
and clothing caught alight, it's very hard going. I've used up
all my sick leave which The Manager says is suspicious.
It is lonely work. She stands in the middle of the office
so everyone can hear and demands: 'why are you so slow?'

CLAIRE CROWTHER

Inwit

The Report said nothing.

It saw the desk approach in measured strides, the desk came on and did not stop. Until a vast edge lipped it, like the sealine on that beach where the Report had lain for perhaps an hour. It had trembled on a promontory, a reddish rock with crumbling margins. There had been eddies of breeze through it. Flutters of pages. Fingers had stroked it, withdrawn, pulled a cross over its whole frontage with damp fingers. Sweat. How much sweat was a part of the Report, those hours of shredding linen, of soaking, of stamping, hanging and drying. The sea had reminisced over a state the Report could not, itself, remember.

The Report said nothing.

The sea withdrew. The Report supposed it had been withdrawn from the beach, carried somewhere. The Report had been incomplete then. It could not fully comprehend its own status. It heard more as the torn legs of winged insects were drawn into shape on its inner leaves. The Report grew from the outside in. It thought more. It crisscrossed its thoughts till they comprehended, it seemed, enough truth and all reason. In the end, it could conclude. That was a realisation light and stark as the ancient elm in winter under which the Report had been left in one incomplete version; excited, bubbling with reference, elegant (it was sure) in its repetitions. The black tracery of elm boughs was so striking that the Report's arguments inhabited it fully, every wrinkling finger and arm of it, every year of its grace, every moment of the Report's disgrace. After which, though the elm was far away, the Report knew its own existence was a loved shadow like a winter tree.

The Report said nothing.

At this moment, lying on the hard breast of a desk, the Report was bereft. Of its role, of its power. Its words were Times New Roman 12 point. Its size was A4. Its pages were deckle edged, rough cut, stressed. Its covers were buckram with an acrylic coating. There was glue inside its spine. A ribbon, sewn from the top of its spine, held a particular page. The Report had become aware of its physical nature once it was placed in an upright position on the desk of its maker. Then, in a kind of darkness, a drawer perhaps, it considered its physical parts. Or had that been a bag stowed on a shelf? Waiting. Till I am born, the Report thought. Its birth had to be borne and was. The journey was comfortable but abrupt. The Report was drawn from the darkness even as a door opened through which its bearer moved, its tall bearer through a high doorframe.

The Report said nothing.

It was tossed as if thoughtlessly, but the Report could think for itself. Of course, it could. It needed no one else now. It could speak for itself. It had the language writhing within it. It had the context. It was prepared. It would be loved by these new communities of formica and wood and steel even as its growth had been loved. And the quiet of the desk, the office, its own office, its official nature, all grew like the power of the silent words – because closed – inside it. The Report would say so much. Exactly so much. It knew there was more than itself, well, how could any report think it was the only report or the begetter of reports. It was, simply, a made thing, a limit of pages, a cut of words, a closable document. It knew all that.

The Report said nothing.

Nothing unknown. It thought, for the first time, that it could only say what had been said. It could only repeat. Elegantly, in that cursive, that sweep, that autumn leave of falling read pages. It could do only what it had been prepared for. But the Report was unsatisfied. It knew itself, how was that? It knew its end, how did it? It could imagine – who knew that? Thinking of that, there was a kind of breath in it. Yet its writer had gone. Had lain it down and gone. Its owner did not hear its breath. Because the Report heard an intake and output of breath. It was somewhere in the centre of its pages, the breath pulled some pages, tightened some words, all of it meant more.

The Report said nothing.

The Report practised the rising intake the falling output. It was drunk with the sensation. The desk surface, so obdurate softened. The light was high and elsewhere grew. Perhaps it was midday. With an enormous effort the Report carried itself upward, till it stood. Covers slightly turned, edges balanced like a dancer on the green leather, ribbon trailing behind as if it had lost its place. It opened itself just a fraction and faced the door.

The Report said:

THEA AYRES

The Authorities

Do you know how long
you've kept me waiting?
I need medical attention.

You know, I've gone off even
the name I chose. I've waited so long,
my own name makes me think of waiting.

Yes, I have ID, but, you see,
I've changed a lot, and there was
an admin error in the first place.

Where am I from? I hardly remember.

You're asking me my story?
I'm not the Transsexual Scheherazade.
Why do you make us wait so long?
I bet if I could pay, I could skip the queue.

Well, okay, if you're the one asking
the questions, why aren't you listening?

My story? Do you know *A Passage to India*?
(Yes, I've read all your literature,
and you've read none of mine.)
Think of yourself as the colonizer, Fielding.
Think of me as Aziz.
I tell you, in the final scene,
we can't be friends till you
renounce your power over me.

No, please stop. Let me keep my clothes.

SHEENAGH PUGH

Other Street

Born on Other Street, they lived according:
never quite the norm, always friendly
to everyone, but somehow keeping

a certain distance. My uncle went to sea
with the merchant service and indulged a flair
for disappearing. No word for years, then suddenly

a postcard from Bombay or Algiers,
some port of longing. Now and then,
the Revenue would write to enquire

if we knew his whereabouts, in vain;
the odd scrawled letter bore no address.
Of course, his death notice is online,

where no-one hides. After all those journeys,
he died no distance from where he set out,
a town like any town in the Valleys.

Now my father, he was no gadabout:
five years of war was enough travel
to last him a lifetime. His escape route

was the library, the grammar school,
the training college. A job for life.
Fifty years married. As dependable

as the town hall clock. Yet every photograph,
near enough, shows a lone foot or arm
whose owner, once again, has made off

just in time, stepping out of the frame
as if he might lose his soul to Kodak.
Later in life, his ears failed him,

or maybe not, for he seemed to draw back
with some alacrity into a state
of silence. Now, following on his track,
I find myself at home on Other Street.

JACQUELINE SAPHRA

Shmattes

These are the rags our foremothers and forefathers
pieced together like prayers in the murk of sweatshops

scraps they shlepped from door to door to earn
something out of nothing   manna for the survivor

food for the kinder who lived to beget my ancestors
of long buried names who begat nevertheless

my great grandmother Sheyna who conjured
by her own hand a yellow dress that caught

the eye of Jack the nice Jewish doctor who married
my grandmother Bessie the Communist who begat

Adrian   Robert   Felicity   and my own mother
Marna the teacher who did not care a button

for the tailor's art but begat me   Yael   I who can
write this poem but barely fix a shmatte to a shmatte

I who begat   Jacob   Tamar   Ethan   Melissa
and therefore by the covenant of these pages

bless and remember   the yellow dress   the thread
the needle   the thimble   luck   feet   donkeys

carts   tracks   trains   courage of crossings
through loss   through fear and storm   the fruit

of the labour   fruit of the dreamer   fruit of the chutzpah
that has kept us alive and brought us to this season.

PHILIP GROSS

What the Thicket Told Me:

Come close, come down, I'll whisper... as the bramble's
        trip-snare meets my misstep and...

        I'm felled
with a spine-shunting slap. The shock
still pulsing through me, after days and nights in pain.

No, bramble didn't do this single-handed – not
        that *single-handed* is a bramble word.

        It was the tangles of nerve
amongst my twigs of bone. If bramble did
call out to them, or they to it, it was the call of like to like

as when a jag of blackthorn, too fine and too deep
        to tease out, was working its hurt,

        an inflammation
simmering, ache of the earth, its
knottedness, its biting back against our trespasses. Its spite.

Unpretty horned rose-briar, barbed wire of bramble,
        choke of strangle-ivy – is that glee

        or rictus on the face
carved up among the gargoyles, grin-
gaping as a conflagration of green flames consume him,

flames he also utters? What if all this, the living-dying
        of the thicket – a bough prostrated,

        grappled down
by ivy, still bristles with twigs, striving
up into leaf and every other branch you lean on snaps

in a hollowed-out fritter of mould – what if this thriving
        into dissolution, each thing in each other,

        is my life too?
No in-here and out-there, no place
to hunker down, in bed, in the dark, that it is not already.

        There is nowhere, least of all inside
        the slack tent of my skin,
        to hide.

PAUL STEPHENSON

Loving the Social Anthropologist I
Romania

He was off doing fieldwork, gone weeks on end,
studying the young men who'd fled to Spain
for work, a rite of passage. What did it mean
for the mothers and sisters and wives left behind
in the emptied out towns of Transylvania?

He collected me in Budapest. I don't recall much:
the parliament, and some party in a bar in the park
to celebrate Mr. Gay Hungary (led there by the friend
of a friend, a ballet dancer we were crashing with),
eight flat hours by train across plains to Romania.

★

Cluj-Napoca was his base. It was arty and buzzing
and I was in his hands. He spoke the language well,
had the weekend planned. We downed shots of ţuică
and I abandoned myself in his rented room, next day
wound through his ravines, his canyons and mountains.

We stopped a night in Baia Mare, had cheap and tasty
pizza and wine. It must have been the randomness
of the place, the fact he was ordering that made me hungry.
I heard his 'da, da… ' and his' 'vă rog', his 'mulţumesc'
watched him nod to the waitress as he chose my topping.

★

In Sighet, on the border with Ukraine, he ran in the mud
from bus to bus to find ours for the Merry Cemetery.
Sitting in the open back, he chatted to the farmhands.
The snow was waist high, and I lost him a while as we
took in the bright blue wooden tombstones. Săpânţa blue.

He translated for me: the man who fell in front of a train,
the three-year old girl hit by a taxi outside her house,
the mother-in-law you mustn't wake in case she bites you.
The accidents, final moments, all shown with cheer,
carving fun out of death with gloss paint and rhyme.

CHRISTODOULOS MAKRIS

the stooges

my friend and Britain jump the shark
in a vegan cafe of entitled rants
she doesn't like him much anymore
we're not together either

he who shall not be named
moves the goalposts so regularly
Christmas in America
must be a delicate strategy
and woos me into collaboration

flattery never fails
even when cheerleader-in-chief resigns
Irish tattler about town

have you considered his immigrant status
was what made him not Arthur
in the office with a riding helmet on
banging the wall lights off
sunny 1950s sets reflecting my village childhood
in odd 30 year recurrences

how I wanted that nickname this love
I could have claimed it by now
create an acronym oh wait
someone jumped the start
that's how friendships slide into harm
not to say empire

I always return to that fight promo
perception manipulator
beating up an army
until strings projections come to be
visible now how nations churn young blood

ruthlessly

swimming in sixteen hours of not very interesting
nevertheless I collect outtakes
when a quote from a woke
approximating this here now
swells their coffers
look
how to articulate
what will I wear that won't make me look
haughty ungrateful
not to say a confidence void
look
woke's not an outfit
much less a noun
the worst tweet in the world
shot out of a padlocked station
until that pest brother-in-law of mine backs off
what a joy it is to live in these times of maximum normality
this must be some kind of cryptic clue
wait what
do I have to uncover
seriously are you talking big time politics
what you leave behind
the putrid smell of bodies
pain and violence the look on a 12 year old
on a photograph from The War
wait you used to be someone to trust
fully in rhyme with my transgressions
I'd call it a white hole of influence
your ignorance now doesn't hurt as much

Making the Past Present

LYNNE HJELMGAARD and PENELOPE SHUTTLE talk to ZOË BRIGLEY about creative partnerships, curiosity, and memory

Zoë Brigley: Lynne, you had this incredible, creative relationship with Dannie Abse, one of our most important Welsh poets. Penny, you had an amazing relationship with the poet Peter Redgrove, but you are also both great writers in your own right with your own geniuses. I suppose I'm also interested in how a creative partnership works. There are many where it does: the Canadian writers Fred Wah and Rita Wong, US poets Vievee Francis and Matthew Olzmann, or British couples Nick Laird and Zadie Smith, or Katie Hale and Loren Cafferty. In Wales, we have Susie Wild and Ben Wildsmith, or Kathryn Gray and Andrew Neilson. But how do you balance a creative relationship with your own sense of creativity and identity? I have a great creative relationship with the poet Kristian Evans, and so this is not an entirely selfless question. [All laugh].

Penelope Shuttle: I think, if you're in the situation, which each of us are, or have been, people seem to project their own expectations and anxieties and feelings on you as a couple. This has absolutely nothing to do with you. It's almost as if it infuriates people that a couple are together writing, and there's a desire to almost to chip away at it, or to be quite antagonistic towards it. That's one thing – people looking at you from the outside.

But as two writers living and working together, you do need to recalibrate consciously a lot of the time. How much time are we spending working together? How much are we working on our own stuff? We had a daughter. During her growing up, it was the division of labour, what each of us was best at. I'm sure, Lynne, you felt this – you have to keep double checking in a supportive way, so you don't get yourself in a situation where somebody's cross all the time because they feel diminished. You have to put a lot of scrutiny into it without losing spontaneity in the relationship.

Lynne Hjelmgaard: It's a bit different for me, because I met Dannie so late in life, and I had been writing already, had published my first book way before I met Dannie. I was very much in the writing scene in Paris, where I lived for six years.

Penelope: Did we meet in France?

Lynne: No, I lived in Paris from the mid-nineties to the beginning of the millennium when my husband was still around. Luckily my husband wasn't a poet. As a matter of fact, he wasn't keen on poetry. My husband and I lived on a boat for many years, and he had this dream that I would write a very romantic novel set on a boat with sex and sailing off into the sunset. [All laugh]. I was in Alice Notley and Douglas Oliver's workshop in Paris, and I would go home and write poems about this life that I had and the life I had left behind. That's where I started in my poetry. It wasn't related to Dannie at all, and in fact, I had never heard of Dannie. We met on an equilibrium, and we didn't have that very close living relationship Penny had with Peter. Though we would meet on the weekends and were close.

Zoë: So, you had that equilibrium, and it just continued into the relationship?

Lynne: I thought that I would just keep doing what I've always been doing. This was in 2008, and I'd been writing for more than 10 years then, publishing my first book, and running around Paris giving readings in bookshops very receptive to Anglophones. I had all that background and energy to take with me, which helped me when I met Dannie, because of course, he had his opinions. He was from more traditional poetry, so we did learn from each other. I was probably more experimental because I'd been studying with Alice, my mentor for many years. I would share my work with Dannie, this 'back and forth' was great. I learned so much from it.

Zoë: I'm also curious about what your creative partnerships were like in a practical way. You were saying that you'd have negotiations, or back and forth about poems. I wonder what that kind of working relationship was like for you both.

Penelope: One of the things we learnt very early on (because obviously we would exchange drafts and critique one another's drafts) was never do it in the house. Never do it in the domestic arena because you have all sorts of domestic issues. Everyone has, so we'd always go out to cafes or in fine weather on park benches. We'd take our paperwork with us, and then you're in a neutral space. That's very freeing. Much as one works against it in in a long-life relationship, you can slip into roles, and that's all part of the negotiating – that you don't stereotype yourself in roles. Going out did make a very clear, creative space, to-ing and fro-ing and critiquing, and affirming one another's work as well. Also having our own areas in the house. It's a long time ago. It's 20 years since Peter died, so I'm reconstructing this from memory. But on the whole, it worked, and when things went off the rails, we worked quite hard to get it back on the rails.

The things we collaborated on… it gives you an insight in how the other person works as well, which also impinges on the whole way of living with someone.

But another element is age. Because Peter was 16 years older than me, and Dannie was older than you, Lynne. That's one of the reasons why I wrote the elegies after Peter died called *Redgrove's Wife*. I wanted the book to be like the seventeenth century, when you referred to someone's wife. But I wanted it to undercut expectations of the gender roles we may or may not have had in the relationship. Because I never used the name Redgrove. The only people who ever called me Mrs. Redgrove were my daughters' teachers at school. You do what you can to not get stereotyped.

We did have a big age gap. People think that the influences are going only one way. But though I met Peter when I was only 22, I'd been publishing prose poem novels since my teens. I wasn't so much writing poems. I was interested in in the possibilities of prose. When we started being together, Peter wrote a novel called *In the Country of the Skin*, and I started to write more poems. It was because we were so curious about one another, at the beginning of a relationship falling in love and learning new things about someone, so we swapped the way we were working.

That's the great advantage of being two writers in a relationship: you can learn from one another, but it was very equal. And, Lynne, this is what I mean about the projection. They see that one person must be the senior person. And the other the less senior, and you know life doesn't work like that. That's not the way you can run a relationship. Well, not one that's going to last.

It's more difficult for people of the same age to live together as writers because of the competitiveness. I had published already. Peter was published, and Lynne and Dannie, you were both published. You weren't competing with one another. The worst possible example of two writers living together is Plath and Hughes, competitive as hell. For people the same age, it's more difficult because of the pressure of getting your publication profile ahead. It's important for both of you to be published. It makes for more harmony.

Lynne: There will always be difficulties and obstacles.

Penelope: There will always need to be recalibration.

Lynne: I just saw the man and the poet. I was recently bereaved, and I heard Dannie read from *The Presence* at Torbay, and it just went right through me. That was my first introduction. There was an honesty, a wisdom, a kindness. It expanded my world without me even having said hello to him. I met him afterwards. I don't know if you were there?

Penelope: Yes, I was there.

Lynne: Yes! I remember him saying "Hi, Penny!" [Both laugh].

Penelope: It was a wonderful reading, and we were all feeling very protective towards him. Because he had recently lost his wife.

Lynne: Yes, but I didn't know anything about him, and I had been traveling a lot, visiting my children. I'd been in Paris visiting friends, and I went to Torbay because my good friend Wendy French was doing a workshop there. So, I was pulling along my suitcase, and I was joking with Dannie: "Do you want to come along in my suitcase?" He was a blessing. A gift.

I didn't know how old he was. I went to his house a couple of days later, when he invited me to lunch, and when I walked into his house, there was this poem of his in a frame on the wall: his birthdate was wrong, as 1931, and I thought, so he's not as old as I thought. That was incorrect, and he was born in 1923. But he was timeless.

Penelope: Yes!

Lynne: We got on the train home together, and I was very shy. I didn't want to show him my work. But, he said, "Wait!", and soon he was showing me drafts of poems he had in his notebooks. When I went to his house, he asked me, "So where are your poems?" Just one of these memories, but he was very curious and receptive to me, and sensitive, because of who he was. It all worked very well, and like Penny said, the idea to meet outside! When I was living in Hampstead, we would meet in Golders Hill Park quite regularly. We would read through my poems. He could see the American influence I had beyond Alice. I inspired him that way too. He would also read me what he was working on.

Penelope: It is always an interchange, isn't it? I first heard Peter when I was 14 years old, on a radio third program, a poem called 'The Case'. It was a 20-minute poem, quite dramatic, and he was reading it. I turned on after it had begun, so I didn't know who it was, and I was absolutely convinced it was a European poet in translation, because it felt so not English. And then it came on it, written and recorded by Peter Redgrove. I was very aware of his work from then but didn't meet him until I was 22 at a friend's house, but it's strange that he made such an impact on me so far back.

Zoë: You both used the word curiosity in different contexts. And I wonder if something important is to have this shared curiosity. For example, recently, Penny, I've been recommending a book you wrote with Peter all about periods, menstruation, and the body: *The Wise Wound*. I absolutely love it. I love that Peter was up for investigating that with you and doing that together.

Penelope: He had a scientist's interest because he started his university as a natural sciences student and then switched to literature. But he'd also had a long training analysis with John Layard who had himself studied with pupils of Jung. So, he'd spent a big part of his life, thinking about Jungian philosophy, along with this interest in natural sciences. When we met, I had a dysfunctional menstrual cycle, physically, emotionally, psychologically, to such an extent that it became quite a stumbling block in living together. I was very young. I was in my twenties, and because of Peter's deep interest in dream interpretation (which is very close to poetry and uses the same kind of muscles of the imagination), we did what people are not supposed to do if they're a couple: a shared analysis through dreams. I did a lot of dream drawings, and we worked on dreams that turned up at times of the cycle which eventually became signposts to dealing with the difficult emotions and factors of my cycle.

So, it was private work of repairing a difficult place in our relationship, and that became the groundwork for *The Wise Wound* which we had not intended to write until, having got to a better place with working on my cycle with dreams, we then went to the literature. We thought there must be lots of books about the psychology of menstruation.

But no, nothing! So we thought we would fill that gap. If the book still has that energy, it's because it came from very difficult personal experience, and a desire to throw light on what was so obscure and difficult, and kept bursting out in in difficult places. As I said, it took us into huge amounts of research on the physiology, and the scientific side. It was very bonding for our relationship because it was the work that we'd done to save ourselves as a couple.

Zoë: Using the difficulty to write something productive seems wonderful.

Penelope: If you can't get round it, you just have to go through it.

Zoë: I find it personally very helpful because premenstrual time is always very difficult for me. There's also the prospect of perimenopause for many of us to be grappling with.

Penelope: The thing for difficult menstruation is dreams and creative writing. Try to write right through it. Find out what is impacting emotional distress and imagine your way through it. Having said that I had a horrible menopause. Peter was diagnosed with Parkinson's during my menopause. I suffered what was called 'reactive depression'. But it's a struggle. It would be a lie to say it isn't.

Zoë: But what about curiosity for you, Lynne?

Lynne: It's such an important ingredient in a relationship. Dannie and I were always looking outwards for other poets, other artists that would inspire us. We would go frequently to the National Museum or the various galleries here in London. He was curious about my work, and I was curious about his. I had been influenced by avant-garde poetry for many years. Dannie introduced me to Edward Thomas. We would read his poems together, and it was just wonderful. Dannie opened me up somehow to other poets, and I opened him. Curiosity is the major ingredient, of writing and reading and everything you do, and that curiosity still drives me to this day. I'm always searching and looking. I have a curiosity about nature. Or maybe it's just the phase that I'm in now.

Of course, there was living on a boat all those years, and being out at sea and living close to Hampstead Heath. I am on the Heath every day and every day I go there, I'm curious. I find something new all the time there. I don't necessarily write about it, but it sparks my curiosity. The world influences me.

Zoë: I love that, and I love that we have moved on to talking about your work specifically. The cartoonist and writer, Alison Bechdel, set up a test where to pass, a movie or text must have two women talking to each other about something other than a man. It's surprising how few movies pass that test. I want this conversation to pass the Bechdel Test and to talk about your poetic geniuses. Let's talk some more about you. You've both had long careers. You both have this curiosity. You both think a lot about nature and the ecological crisis. We talked a bit about this in your #HowIWriteAPoem feature on the *Poetry Wales* website, didn't we, Penny?

Penelope: Well, Lynne and I would have read when it came out, Rachel Carson's *Silent Spring*. For us, none of this is news. It's been part what impacts you as a person and as a writer. It's wonderful to see so much focus being put on poems that are specifically writing from an ecological point of view. But it's not new. We're in the middle right now [September 2023] of a ridiculous, dangerous heat wave. This is not normal. This is not a nice end to summer. This is wrong. This is the manifestation of global warming right in front of us. I suppose there has been an increased immediacy that's built on this: knowing since the 1960s that we're losing species. It's been lurking in our work for a long time. But certainly extinction, which was warned about by Rachel Carlson as something that would happen … we're dealing with that now. It has happened and is happening very presently. It is that very present feeling of increased danger that we're writing from.

I've always liked writing about animals, their energies and symbolism as well as their realities being important to me. In the piece 'More' in the #HowIWriteAPoem series, my poem says we need more animals, not less. I'm writing currently, in my work-in-progress, *History of the Child*, from the perspective of a nine-year-old child, which is partly me but also a transpersonal child. Children have great affinity with animals. I'm also writing sestudes.

Lynne: Sestudes?

Penelope: The sestude was devised by a guy called John Simmons for the 26 Collective, and they had a project where they went into the V&A Museum in London, and each writer chose an object, and they wrote a sestude about it. A sestude is a poem that is 62 words only minus the title and any footnotes. I've just loved doing them. I was asked originally to write two sestudes as part of a project on places in Cornwall. I was given Saint Feock, one of the Cornish saints, and instead of writing two sestudes, I wrote an alphabet of them for him. I am very addicted. [Laughs.]

Zoë: I do like the short poem, and they're quite hard to write.

Lynne: Yes!

Zoë: There must be something in it which grips you. In fact, in this issue we have a feature on good short poems. The short poem can be wonderful.

Penelope: I like sequences as well, and if you can find one thematic umbrella, I think a sequence is lovely, taking the short poem on a kind of trip.

Lynne: Sometimes you can just take two lines and then expand them. Besides looking out towards nature and looking out towards the world. I also look in, and I use my journals a lot when I'm looking for lines that have some sort of energy to them. I have a whole closet full of journals going back more than 20 years. I don't know what I'm going to do with them. And I don't want my kids reading them. [All laugh].

The last month or two has been sort of a blank time for me. I keep telling myself, "Well, that's all right, I don't have to keep generating good poems, or even a poem". I look in my journals, and there's nothing going on here. But that's okay. The empty space is good.

Penelope: It is important to just to step back sometimes and either go into nature or to reading. The waiting is quite important sometimes, and it's a really fulfilling space sometimes. And when I return into writing, I really feel reenergized.

Zoë: I used to journal like years ago, before I got married, before having children and divorce. I went back and looked at those journals recently, and I thought, this is quite interesting. Perhaps I should start it up again. Sometimes life gets in the way, doesn't it?

Lynne: It gets in the way, but it also puts you there – puts you in the way.

Penelope: I stopped keeping journals, because I did them sporadically for years and years, and it's true. I go back into them, and the phrases will leap out at you. I don't regret stopping, because it became a kind of tyranny, and you do things when they work for you, don't you? Years and years I used to keep journals of my dreams.

Lynne: Yes! I did too.

Penelope: I look at the dream journals, and they don't really give that energising phrase the way the journals do. Occasionally I'll have a dream that has the immediacy that will go into a poem. I suppose for some people it's morning pages, isn't it? That's what Katrina Naomi does.

Lynne: I don't do them so religiously anymore.

Penelope: I have phases when they're useful.

Lynne: Sometimes, you can be lucky with a poem, and it will just come. I had a dream about my sister, not that long ago, she passed away about a year ago. I woke up from the dream, and the poem was all there.

Penelope: That doesn't happen unless the rest of the time you're keeping that channel open with the imagination, living with language. So you're ready for that poem when it when it comes.

Lynne: Well, this was six months ago. I think I was just very much in touch with my sister, and she was so real in this dream, and everything that happened in the dream was just her. I had to write it down. I believe that it was a real interaction with her. I hadn't been sleeping for the longest. Up until then, I was just really having a hard time, and in that dream, we had said our goodbyes. I really believe that.

Penelope: Saying goodbye is so difficult.

Lynne: Saying goodbye in this dream. And then it became this poem.

Penelope: She gave you that!

Zoë: For both of you, remembering is important. So, Penny, you're writing about childhood, and in Lynne's new book *The Turpentine Tree,* there are memories of people.

Lynne: That's where the energy comes from: people that I know, that have been important in my life. It's finding a place for them somehow. The new book is dedicated to my grandchildren. I don't see them very much, but they're there, and I want to bring them closer, making them present.

Penelope: Memory, and far memories from childhood struck me, and one of the reasons I began to write along this path is the sheer randomness of what you remember and what you forget. Why is one of the poems about a girl I went to school with, and was not a particularly close friend with? Her parents had a farm, but because it was suburban, and quite near London, where I was brought up at Staines, the farm abutted on to some common land. Just this little leftover farm, and why that popped back up into my memory and led me onto exploring things - there's no explanation for it. But something made that little nexus of memory last. Whereas I can look back into childhood's other areas, and there's just darkness and gaps. And then there's one thing that comes and switches on its light. The randomness and strangeness of memory was one of the elements that led me to go back and write about childhood, though a lot of it is completely invented as well. There's the memory cycle. And then there's the invented transpersonal childhood experiences.

The difference is between voluntary and involuntary memory. It's an engaging area for me now, and a lot of it is sparked because my mother died almost two years ago. My mother was a hundred years old when she died, and she had her retained all her cognition throughout her elder years until the last few weeks of her life, because she had cancer, and that takes everything away from you at the end. For a long time, I had my mother, with all her memories intact and her personality undiminished. When she went, that really intensified my feelings about looking back, even though she doesn't really appear in any of these poems. But childhood obviously connects me to my mum.

Six Poems by FABIO MORÁBITO
Translated by RICHARD GWYN

1. There are trees that are born for the forest

There are trees that are born for the forest
and others that are a forest without knowing it.
The tree ignores the forest
and perhaps the forest ignores the tree,
all we know is the root that rummages
and the branch that also rummages,
one in its sky of mud,
the other in its sky of cloud.
Life is rummaging, and to each of us our sky.

2. In Antarctica

In Antarctica
pelts do not flourish.

The bear never came here,
nor the wolf, the musk ox.

The heartbeat was protected
beneath a heavy layer of fat,

the fat that surrounds forms,
and round forms prefer water.

How ungainly their movements on the ground,
the penguin and the walrus.

So much ineptitude in Antarctica,
so many circus somersaults.

Antarctica and the fat of its seals,
Antarctica and the plumage of its birds.

The pelt has not prospered
and in the air flight is free,

without the hindrance of trees and fruits,
the smells that stir the appetite.

Nothing is hidden in Antarctica,
there is no lying in wait, only distance,

they hunt in packs,
they flee in herd and shoal,

they live and die crowded close
and agony is unknown.

In winter, before the sea freezes,
fat abandons Antarctica.

Only the penguin remains,
setting out on his march,

moving far from the sea,
and for once only

an incredible line of tracks
crosses the slab of ice.

And for once only, where everything is erased,
there remains a furrow, a visible longing

that allows Antarctica
to fully emerge.

3. I write prose while gathering courage

I write prose while gathering
courage to write verse,
I write prose so that the poems
can almost write themselves,
I write prose like one who drives
an ox to plough a field.

All that prose to gather
courage for the poems,
all those words dragged by force
to the end of every phrase,
all those straight lines
because I didn't know how to leave the furrow.

4. I am the last person

I am the last person,
the last speaker of a language, my own,
that hangs entirely on my tongue,
a complete heritage of words
that will fall into oblivion
the day I breathe my last,
the language that I speak to myself and that I forget
because it has ceased to be a language and is only a heritage.
Many of its words are already dead
because I will not utter them again,
and even if I say them, everything that I say,
for lack of anyone who understands me,
is my own invention, despite my words resembling
in every detail the words I learned as a child,
and sometimes I wonder if we are not all
the last speakers of the things we say.

5. And if the fruit no longer gave itself?

And if the fruit no longer gave itself?
If it stopped hanging from the trees
and ripening on the ground?
If there were no more citrus
or even nuts?
What would become of our arms,
of our famous thumbs,
born to pluck?
All distances
were born from the fruit
that we must pick
on the next branch,
on the nearby tree,
in the adjoining forest,
in the tribe across the river.
Fruit drove us onward,
scattered us from the start.
Behind every luxury,
every desire,
every journey – its sweetness.
Meat too we eat like fruit
and not like meat,
we pluck it from a flock of meat
as the ripest fruit is plucked,
all that is succulent

falls into our mouths
as if shaken from a branch,
like you, who I pluck each day
from your tree, from your tribe
and bring you to this side of the river
and eat you and bite you and keep you
and fear that you will rot.

6. As I wait for you

As I wait for you, I would like
to put a chair out on the street,
but nowadays no one puts
chairs out on the street.
There was a chair in my house
whose purpose was just that,
it was kept in a place apart,
no other chair went out except for it.
The chair for putting on the street.

Just Your Imagination

CHRISTODOULOS MAKRIS investigates the case of the ~~absent~~ elusive Irish avant-garde

Defining a poetic avant-garde, like defining the terms 'experimental' or 'innovative' in poetry – often misappropriated or employed as interchangeable – is an ever-shifting conversation with no conclusion or consensus. It is in this impossibility of consensus, summary or categorisation, in this lack of ready answers but in the questions themselves, that the essence of an imaginary definition may lie. Disparate poets, groups, initiatives and movements occasionally appear in ephemeral bursts of activity lighting a path for anyone searching for long-term engagement with what poetry can do beyond its traditionally understood function. Despite or perhaps as a consequence of many contemporary poets and writers claiming experimental status, the term has become almost meaningless except as something like a promotional label. Rather than producing something 'absurd' or 'odd' within the traditional parameters of poetry, experimentalism as a prelude to an avant practice tends to inhere in an approach rather than a type of content, and in embracing the existential crisis of the artform – attitudes enacting an interrogation of intention, context and language use in all its forms, testing, blurring or ignoring labels and boundaries regarding genre, privileging process over product, or undermining expectations from consumers of poetry to derive linear or conclusive meaning.

On 7 July 2009, Wurm im Apfel, a pioneering platform for live experimental poetry events and small independent press founded by Kit Fryatt and Dylan Harris in Dublin, and which having operated roughly between 2008 and 2016 is now on a prolonged hiatus, hosted a performance by Dutch sound poet Jaap Blonk. Despite representing a remarkable intervention in the Irish poetry landscape, the performance was witnessed by a small number of people, several of whom were temporary visitors to the city who happened to recognise the profile of the poet. The relative apathy to this event may be explained by the almost absolute value that continues to be bestowed on traditional book publication of 'collections' of poems with 'recognised' presses, and with the performance of poetry generally understood either as a recitation of previously published poems, or in 'spoken word' terms which privilege the transfer of meaning from performer to audience in ways that seek to convince, self-fortify, or include through a shared social, political or philosophical outlook, and which therefore rely on tried and tested tools (the 'poetry voice', consolidated gesture, wordy introduction, and so on) consequently resulting in conservative poetic forms.

Examples of sound poetry, improvisational poetics or other modes blending sound, poetry and performance have remained rare in Ireland, or have predominantly emerged in cross-pollination with other artforms. The poetry-as-performance-art (or performance-art-as-poetry) of James King has consistently embedded pre-lingual, guttural, gestural, or phonetic elements calling attention to the spaces and relationships between language as communication tool and its physical mark on a page, body, place, as well as the endurance capabilities of the poet. Aodán McCardle has worked for many years in the realms of performance writing/drawing, improvisation, and creating audiovisual atmospheres to explore how poetry may be articulated through physicality. Suzanne Walsh, in their capacity as a multidisciplinary artist working through sound, performance and text, regularly blends vocal performance, field sounds and found text in sometimes site-specific sonic interventions. In pure sound poetry terms, 'Dublin

Onion,' a score for two voices composed by Cah-44 and regularly performed in collaboration with Raven in spoken word circles at the beginning of the 2010s, is a vibrant and conceptually tight work transcending the limitations of the spoken word format, merging language, sound, place and performance.

When it comes to visual poetics the ground is barely more fertile despite the fact that visual poetry may be represented through traditional book publication. Susan Connolly remains one of very few poets in Ireland working consistently in visual or concrete poetry, her work having appeared in publication for nearly two decades across a number of presses including Shearsman and Redfoxpress. 'Confetti', an ongoing project by Bebe Ashley, makes use of 3D printing technology to manufacture lines of poetry printed in Braille – a combination of visual and 3D object poetry performed through intersemiotic translation to explore issues of accessibility.

To understand the poetic character of the above works is to accept that poetry need not be destined for the page or its digital approximation, or hold a linear verbal meaning, or indeed impart meaning in a way that puts the content of the poem front and centre as its undisputed product. In October 2021 the online journal *Honest Ulsterman* published 'Glossolalia', an audiovisual poem by Hayley Carr, in the form of an embedded video depicting Carr performing the poem. Given the nature of *Honest Ulsterman* – in common with the majority of online literary journals – as a digital outlet approximating a print journal, its readers expect to read work published on it in 'flat' textual terms. 'Glossolalia' appeared unmoored from its surroundings, with its multidimensional conceptual play on backmasking, including an embedded connection to the poet's family history, remaining uncontextualised, without hints or tools towards its exploration (except via a note on the poet's YouTube channel) and therefore essentially unread.

Multifariousness of poetic medium is a core element in the ambitious *MOTHERBABYHOME* project by Kimberly Campanello, which exists in a number of formats: as a 796-page reader's edition (a book) and as a poetic object (printed on transparent vellum and held in an oak box), both published by zimZalla in 2019; as a digitally documented performance (through the Irish Poetry Reading Archive at University College Dublin); and as a one-off, undocumented durational performance (at Oonagh Young Gallery, Dublin, in April 2019). That *MOTHERBABYHOME* stands as an accomplished example of a poetic report, tightly conceived and delivered through a combination of documentary, conceptual and visual poetics – a rigorous response to historical abuses related to the Mother and Baby Home operated in Tuam, Co Galway by the Bon Secours Sisters on behalf of the Irish State between 1926 and 1961, and which resulted in the death of 796 infants and children, with visible emotional impact on readers, audiences, and the poet herself during performances – points to the barely tapped potential of avant poetics to be theoretically and intellectually sound, moving, and socially 'relevant' simultaneously.

The advent of the internet and in particular the proliferation of widely available compositional tools through personal computing has made the digital space ripe for exploration as a multidimensional poetic medium. Since the Covid lockdowns of 2020 and the subsequent prevalence of Zoom or equivalent platforms as sites of gathering, we have witnessed festivals and events transferring themselves onto the digital space while trying to replicate the experience of being in the same room, making a virtue of the expanded access offered by the online forum. However the potential of the digital medium and what it can add to poetry in terms of modes of composition as well as performance has remained relatively unexplored. The possibilities of digital publishing with respect to time, space and depth can give even simple poetic ideas remarkable dimensions: Graham Allen's *Holes*, a project consisting of a ten-syllable line of poetry contributed each and every day since 23 December 2006, has gathered attention as a fusion of the lyrical and the digital, and as an early innovative adoption of digital poetics in Ireland. More recently, *sorry that you were not moved*, a collaborative digital publication by Kimberly Campanello and myself, appears as an interactive 'book' of poetry that not only exists but was also specifically conceived and composed to operate as a navigable website incorporating text, image (still and moving) and sound.

Navigable poetry in physical spaces has existed well before the internet of course, but in the post-internet era such formats gesture towards the gaps and connections between digital and physical, and their relationships to the poetic at both the compositional and reading moments. In the same way that digital readers may toggle between the locations that comprise the poetic spaces in *sorry that you were not moved*, attendees were also able to move, physically in those cases, among the texts of Alice Lyons' public art installation *Staircase Poems* in The Dock, Carrick-on-Shannon, Co Leitrim (2005-6), and Julie Morrissy's *Positions Gendered Male in Bunreacht na hÉireann | 1937 Constitution of Ireland* during TULCA Festival of Visual Arts 2020 in Galway's An Post Gallery. The impermanence of these works, existing in their particular forms, times and spaces (and now accessible only through documentation) contributed the element of ephemerality to their reading, each encounter producing a different sensation or response in each reader on each different occasion, posing questions on the nature of language as assumed carrier of concrete or inflexible meaning.

Interactions between poets and audiences do not necessarily flow one way – indeed, contemporary conditions of living and communication are increasingly multidirectional, obliging any artistic initiative purporting to operate in avant modes to perform at the very least a partial internalising of these conditions. Festivals, events or other happenings with an inherent understanding of this dynamic can provide fertile ground for poetic conversations that dissolve barriers between poets and audiences, constructing something communally enduring. For 20 years (1997-2017) SoundEye Festival in Cork held a prominent role in collecting strands of a poetic avant-garde in Ireland, drawing on the directorial efforts of Trevor Joyce initially, and subsequently of Fergal Gaynor, Jimmy Cummins, Rachel Warriner and others, extending outwards in terms of artform and with a decidedly international remit. Aiming to define an avant-garde is inevitably a counterproductive exercise as the term is essentially slippery and intangible: it represents an approach, a stance on artistic endeavour that moves faster than its individual practitioners have the capacity to evolve. As exemplified by SoundEye, this suggests that closed-circuit, short-term or one-off events and happenings tend to come closest to capturing an energy that could then be harnessed towards future moveable iterations. 'Yes But Are We Enemies' was a 10-day touring project I produced and curated in collaboration with English poet and artist SJ Fowler in September 2014 as the invited international extension of Fowler's Enemies Project to Ireland, showcasing specially-commissioned, experimentally-minded collaborative poetry in performance. 'TEXT/SOUND/PERFORMANCE' was a 3-day conference that took place in April 2019, rooted in University College Dublin (UCD) but extending into other institutional spaces. Directed by Gregory Betts, visiting Craig Dobbin Professor of Canadian Studies at UCD in 2018-19, 'TEXT/SOUND/PERFORMANCE' was, as Betts subsequently wrote to me in an email, "less an intervention in Ireland than a spill over from happenings in Canada that found fertile ground in the country".

According to Betts, the biggest impact of TEXT/SOUND/PERFORMANCE was on the published form of avant-garde literature, citing the small press culture of gift exchange, with experimental poetry's irreverent attitude often finding expression in liberated or decentralised spaces for publication. This is where some recent development may be seen in Ireland, but it should be noted that such spaces are, by their very nature and lack of institutional support, either involuntarily ephemeral or fitful, dependent on the (finite) efforts and energy of individuals, or labelling themselves experimental or avant without the reality tallying with the claim.

Some of these publishing operations may indeed view the more transgressive material produced by poets associated with Ireland, some of which strays from the accepted realm of (verbal) poetry altogether, as beyond the pale. Robert Herbert McClean's *Songs for Ireland* (Prototype, 2019) not only enacts a brutal repudiation of official or state-sanctioned poetic culture, but does so in a cartoonish, formally uncategorisable, relentlessly witty manner variously using multimedia elements and hallucinatory polyvocal interventions. Existing simultaneously as fragments of in-your-face video pieces, McClean's work holds a unique and perhaps necessarily alienated position within Irish poetry, and transmits a sense that poetry as commonly understood may not be fit-for-purpose.

The spill over effect of 'TEXT/SOUND/PERFORMANCE' can be understood as another strand in the collection of approaches that may define an avant poetic practice, privileging formal and cultural hybridity and the crossing of nation state boundaries, in the process bringing into effect or aiding an outwardness that is a foundational element of progressive poetries. The generation of poets working in experimental modes who came into artistic maturity before the turn of the millennium, and who have been celebrated more generously in non-Irish territories than 'at home' – poets such as Maurice Scully, Catherine Walsh, Billy Mills, Trevor Joyce – have operated as 'Irish poets' in cultural spaces beyond the officially sanctioned to produce work that revels in pluralism, linguistic flexibility, a refusal to conform to linearity of thought or a workshopping culture with its insistence on the cause-and-effect poem or the single-page/under-40 line piece as the de facto unit of poetry.

As in the much-exploited cases of the international historical avant-gardes of Joyce and Beckett, many of the poets and writers associated with Ireland – including those who resist being formally labelled as such – who push formal and procedural boundaries have either made their work elsewhere or operate in Irish poetic spaces having arrived from elsewhere. Over the past two decades Philip Terry has produced a remarkable body of work in poetry and prose rooted in the Oulipian modes of constrained writing and potential literatures from his base in Essex. Back in Ireland, Nidhi Zak/Aria Eipe's debut book of poetry *Auguries of a Minor God* (Faber & Faber, 2021) has in parts adopted an innovative approach to form and typography, and includes an epic abecedarian poem in the structure of a Fibonacci sequence to illuminate aspects of the migrant experience. And in choosing to publish her second book of poetry with a title in Greek which the vast majority of her readers in Ireland would not be able to read or pronounce, Dimitra Xidous invites us to consider the in-between spaces of cultural and linguistic experience, and how the hyphenation and circularisation of cultural existence may yield experiences and pleasures, intellectual and bodily, beyond the reach of the parochial or monocultural creature.

Ellen Dillon's *Morsel May Sleep* (Sublunary Editions, 2021) performs an exploration of the possibilities of radical translation and language-in-flux speaking across time and influence, while her *Butter Intervention* (Veer2, 2022) makes use of pre-existing material in ways that puts into perspective the many other projects recently appeared in Ireland that dip their toe in documentary poetics. What Ailbhe Darcy described in issue 132 of

Poetry Ireland Review (December 2020) as a "tiny explosion of documentary works in Irish poetry" has coincided with 'The Decade of Centenaries Programme 2012-2023' sponsored by The Department of Tourism, Culture, Arts, Gaeltacht, Sport and Media. In evidence has been an increase in often institutionally-sanctioned engagement with archival material, which has inevitably given rise to much opportunistic work that often fails to engage with the radical possibilities of documentary poetics. The continued heavy reliance on the lyric, personal experience, and the guiding authorial voice, as opposed to a more nuanced authorial presence that makes use of a compositional approach privileging the exclusive arrangement of the documentary material itself, dilutes the potential of much of this work.

There is a growing understanding that poets who perform a crossover in roles including curatorship or creative collaboration in truly self-effacing terms allow a distancing from themselves and develop an unhierarchical outlook that has a liberating effect on the entirety of their work. Kit Fryatt's practice has assumed many guises over twenty years or so – as poet, editor, publisher, teacher, performer and curator. His work performs a flux in language, identity and poetic effect in the time-honoured yet profoundly refreshing 'show, don't tell' mode. The presence of his work in the anthology *Queering the Green* (The Lifeboat Press, 2021) as one of a handful of examples operating broadly within avant poetics speaks to the potential of queer poetries – in comradeship with other marginalised identity poetries – as the site of a formally and conceptually radical poetics extending beyond the expression of selfhood through the lyric mode, or the presumed authority of the poet's voice. Indeed, such traditional modes of writing may sit uncomfortably within the subversive remit of LGBTQ+, feminist, migrant, PGM (people of the global majority) and other hitherto marginalised poetries, as they tend to perpetuate the traditional imperial and patriarchal powers that brought into dominance these imbalances in the first place.

What Gregory Betts identifies as the development of a small press culture in Ireland since 2019 is tempered by the temporality of many of these initiatives, but also the appropriation of the term experimental or avant-garde as a vague signifier of cool. Nevertheless a small number of such presses, counter-intuitively operating beyond urban centres, have been issuing remarkable bodies of work, some for a sustained period of time, and with a readership and support scattered predominantly beyond Ireland. Erica van Horn and Simon Cutts' Coracle Press based in a South Tipperary farm has been in operation for several decades and defines its concerns as residing with "the mechanisms of the book as a manifestation of the poem itself". Francis Van Maele's Redfoxpress in Achill Island, Co Mayo, has been a fiercely outward-looking international press publishing visual poetry books through its "c'est mon dada" series, as well as artists' books and fluxus & assembling boxes among more. Gorse Editions, the imprint of *gorse* journal as interconnected publishing operations with the tagline 'art in words' – and where I have served as poetry editor since 2014 – published as its inaugural title a book of poetry by Ailbhe Darcy and SJ Fowler: *Subcritical Tests* (2017) came about as an extension of Darcy and Fowler's collaborations that developed during the 'Yes But Are We Enemies' tour, and experiments with the joint authorship model with each line in each poem belonging to both and neither. Poetry in experimental collaboration as a device towards decentralisation and destabilisation of the poetic ego, effecting a liberating distancing from the often obsessively personal themes that poets find themselves drawn towards, gestures perhaps more than any other mode towards an understanding of the briefly intense, collective and exploratory spaces a contemporary avant garde may take as its operating milieu.

Led by the technological changes delivered at a dizzying pace over the past thirty years and which have blurred all sorts of boundaries in terms of identity, culture, reading/publishing media, intellectual ownership, human/artificial intelligence, and truth/fiction, the act of reading itself and the digital gesture have emerged as radically commonplace forms of critical creativity. The potential of self-creation and identity-flexibility in online and increasingly in physical and legal spaces has made concrete the resonance of writing in a range of personas as an embodiment of personal-authorial fragmentation and dispersal, reflecting the widespread explicit or implicit act of identity (re)branding and performance.

We begin to recognise the imaginary or absent, or maybe more accurately elusive, Irish poetic avant garde as a messy conglomeration of threads, initiatives, projects and activities that sometimes interact but which don't necessarily fit together as a unified scene. Rather they operate in a disparate fashion to undermine the notion of a singular or hierarchical poetic culture and to embrace the breakdown of the significance of the poet as a traditional figure of authority. Such circularity of influence, discussion, argument and constant interplay of progression and regression, the questioning and reanimating of artistic, cultural, technological, personal, and other perpetually contested spaces, and the never-ending subsumption of the old into the new, with – in a healthy and mature society – each new generation instantly usurping and re-influencing the old, are what might potentially characterise, though not define, an avant garde in the poetry of Ireland or indeed elsewhere.

SOPHIA RUBINA CHARALAMBOUS

Game Bird

On their lunch hour, yiayia and pappou plucked
pheasants in the garden. Their guy would bring
two black bags and a wad of cash round the back.
Pappou dragged those two swollen sacks across
concrete steps to the corner of the garden covered
by a plastic roof. They would take turns to work
on stripping every feather off those brown birds'
cold bodies. Their technique was to clump and
pull in the opposite direction from growth until
what remained were sad black spots on pale skin.
Pappou's calloused hands savoured the job more
than his face as he steadily increased his speed,
adding birds to the pile with a lack of sentiment.
He always left yiayia to finish the job, to return
to the sewing machine where he felt less foreign.
Yiayia continued until a heap of naked birds lay
peacefully on unplastered patio. Out of each one
she picked shot shells buried in their flesh. As
they came out she listened to their familiar clink
on the ground when she threw them to the floor,
her muscles remembered what the brain erased,
that if you leave during war, your homeland does
not want you back. Yiayia seemed to enjoy it most,
sitting wide-legged on a stool, her feet submerged
in feathers. When they caught the wind, they blew
up into hair and formed a nest. She kept plucking
even when feathers stuck to the sweat on her brow,
chest, the gap between her eyes and glasses. Yiayia
rose up, out of the plumage, a pheasant. She turned
into the bird, with wings that can never fly away.

CHAUCER CAMERON

O Glaslyn – Later we will fly

It isn't in the way she moves, for she is grouse, or pleads her case to be.
But even so, a grouse is still a grouse and she is my love –
brighter, better, in her tight-fitted burgundy coat.

She hates cars. I once saw a scrap of her hidden beneath
coarse-woody stems of autumn ling heather, and the sight
of such tightly clustered purple-pink flowers brought me to tears.

She won't admit the terrestrial part of her gait.
Once halfway up, she stopped and said, *later we will fly*
leaving me waiting on the landing, a blur of tumbleweed floating in my eyes.

She is quiet, so quiet she is silent
and every analogue clock
in the house has been smashed for its tick.

It isn't the way she spills lime juice and honey
sometimes deliberately letting it drip from her spoon.
It lingers in strands, hovers over the deep-pile white carpet.

She has blue eyes that do not need describing, other than they are not grey.
She almost left me once for saying grey. They are as clear today
as the first time we met, despite the rain, despite amen, despite the priest –

Abdulkareem Abdulkareem Frontier III
Duplex (Lotus)

I'm imperfect, the opposite of a lotus flower.
I'm white as the moon, dark as the night; colour of twilight.

> Daylight or darkness or the colour of twilight.
> Some days, I spare the roaches & I spare the ants.

& some, I don't spare the roaches & I don't spare the ants.
Some days, I hold on to remorse, the size of a raindrop.

> Some days, I hold on to remorse, wide as my country.
> The girl on WhatsApp calls me a good man.

But what makes a man worthy of being good?
I am learning to avoid things that unearth my flaws.

> My flaw is a diorama designed with colourless things.
> I hold on to my anger like a slow violence.

My anger holds on to me like a slow violence.
I'm imperfect, the opposite of a lotus flower.

BEN RHYS PALMER

Adrian Street Meets GIs, Brynmawr, 1943

Their tanks and trucks come rolling up Windsor
Road. Locals fly Stars and Stripes, Union Jacks,
in love already with the Yanks' breezy glamour.
Cash-flashing hotshots, trading banter and gags,
with waves for the kids, winks for the belles.
"Give us some gum, chum," the children chant.
The soldiers toss packets, sparking mad scrambles.
Adrian – just three, tiny – gets diddly-squat.
But he's spotted by one GI, leaning on a wall,
chatting up the butcher's daughter. He calls him over,
places a perfect white cube into Adrian's paw.
"It's sugar, kid. You can eat it." A cube of sugar!
Adrian's never seen such an exquisite thing.
He touches it gently, just once, to his tongue.

Note: From a sonnet sequence about Adrian Street, a coalminer's son who quit Benyon's Colliery when he was 16 to become a flamboyant, androgynous international wrestling star, helping to inspire glam rock in the process. Adrian passed away in July 2023 at the age of 82.

RICHARD MARGGRAF TURLEY

Gas Masks

We disturbed them in the attic
stowed beneath magazines and puzzles,
sensing the air thicken,
taking turns to run fingers
over khaki stockinette
and black rubber,
elephant-trunk hoses stiff and alien,
holding the facepieces like relics,
donning them as new recruits,
thumbs raw under elastic,
digging in our chins
till the harness tightened.

Still ghostly, the weight
of canvas haversack
strapped to my chest, the give
of the button-down flap,
the thump of blood in my ears,
your oval lip aged solid
as wire gauze and cotton pad,
as a charcoal heart –
you looking out through
thread-less eyes
at what we'd done,
insulated, alert to the mess.

JOSHUA SEIGAL

Here We All Are

My great-grandfather came over from Odessa
packed into a box in the hold of a ship,
with nothing but a hole through which to breathe.

He had a wife he hated, who hated him,
and they set up a shop in the valleys of South Wales.
Above it, they slept in separate rooms.

When he laughed he made *lokshen* come out of his nose.
His wife had fled the Nazis just before the war,
but her polio meant she could never catch my grandpa

or Aunty Helen when they were naughty.
Digging one day in the family archives, my dad
discovered that my great-grandfather and his wife

were also uncle and niece. Grandpa said that
should this ever get out, he'd never speak to my dad again.
He bore his shame silently, like a lump in the throat

that could not be got rid of. He'd take tots of vodka
when he thought we weren't watching,
and although he claimed not to believe in God

he prayed fervently every night, just in case.
All the books on his shelves were about Hitler
or the Jews, and one time he swore he saw a ghost.

And like a ship the dread traverses generations,
criss-crossing the strata back and forth, from
my sister refusing to go to school to me huddled tight

in the doctor's room; from my mum with a husband
who doesn't understand to my brother
who vanished across the world. Here I am

in a box of my own. Here we all are, trying to breathe,
packed tight together, reaching through holes
as our ghost ship lurches on endless seas.

BILLY RAMSELL

Some fraying to spine tips
Barcelona 1830, 2003

She hears her father, in the drawing room,
expound on his three nemeses:
Madrid, the French,
free trade in the textile industry.

She hears a carriage beneath her balcony
clipping slowly along Ferran Street,
to where the half-finished boulevard surrenders,
is devoured by lanes and tenements.

> *A large octavo volume.*
> *Bound in green calf leather.*
> *Preserving the original gilt-lettered spine.*

She watches dust motes in concert hovering
about her teal boudoir.
She settles at her escritoire,
inclines her head above the dictionary.

She caresses a cream, tight-printed column:
Calabós, Cantimplora, Carxofa
Now there's a word she's never seen written down.
Carxofa. One of her grandmother's words.

> *Pere Labèrnia's*
> *First Printed Dictionary*
> *of the Catalan Tongue.*

It is something, she thinks in hard-edged gratitude.
It is something for a *senyoreta*
to be gifted such a fern-green volume,
to cradle an entire language.

Even a reborn, half-tolerated language,
such as this one in 1830,
that has as yet commissioned no sonneteers,
set no epic drifting on the *Midi.*

> *Some fraying to spine tips.*
> *Hinges weak with slight give.*
> *Covers still firmly attached.*

She hears her father offering brandy
from his estate in the middle Penedès.
Peace with England, war with everyone else
she hears swarthy Ermegnol exclaim.

Ermegnol, her father's *agent d'affaires*,
who fought in the occupation,
who, she has been given to infer,
would make a most acceptable intended.

> *With 1830 ownership signature*
> *-Agnès Cenas i Bonaplata-*
> *in ink upon its endpapers.*

Look! A coral-coloured adjective
comes fluttering from the covers,
perches restless at her elbow;
and then a silver-beaked abstraction

slips from the fragrant pages too
to be followed by a dove of sorts,
pearl-pale, interrogative,
that hums and hovers about her temples.

> *Fine. In a near fine slipcase.*
> *Clean overall and bright internally.*
> *Uncommon in this condition.*

TANGIE MITCHELL offers a Poetry Workshop on Nightlife, Love and (Be)Longing

In what ways does a club or bar act as a site of transformative encounter? How does nightlife – a beloved dive bar filled with regulars or a frequented nightclub, packed wall to wall with lovers, friends, and beautiful strangers – engender experiences of freedom, belonging, or desire? What is the role of the club or bar as sanctuary, as community gathering place, especially for queer folks and others with marginalized identities? Considering craft, how do poets use nightlife as an entry point to explore romance, transformation, liberation, and the complexities of human relationships?

The city and urban life, which according to poet Rigoberto González is "fraught with desire and anxiety," has long been a fixation for poets. Writing about nightlife is an extension of this tradition of the poet and the city, our urgent need to understand our place in it. As the sun fades, our day jobs end, our daily distractions paused in the stillness of the night, the city's underbelly surfaces and the poet may find themself unmoored, alone; in need of love, connection; drifting, curious; restless and often ravenous. Cue the downtown dance club with its glittered floor and metallic walls; the small local bar with its wooden stools that creak under our weight, its blaring jukebox's impressive collection of deep cuts; cue the well-hidden speakeasy with its live jazz band and chandelier lights dimmed almost to darkness. Cue the night and our crawling through it.

For this workshop, we'll look more closely at our own brushes with nightlife, however grand or small, and consider what those moments meant for our interiority. How did you end up there? What were you looking for? Did you go alone? Were you in your hometown or a different city, country? What did you learn about yourself that night? What did you learn about others?

To help guide us, we'll first look at three poems that utilize the speakers' nightlife experiences as points of self-discovery. Let's start with John Keene's 'Playland.' Here, the speaker casually walks into a gay bar in Boston, 'emboldened finally / by boredom...' He has gone alone, taking in the bar's sounds (a jukebox 'serenading / us with Kool & the Gang') and patrons in vibrant detail.

> a sundry row
> of torsos, bandaged in striped acrylic knits
> or belted jackets from the 1970s

Despite being in a new place without his 'crew,' notice this moment of realization and transformation for the speaker: 'For once / my anonymity made me feel serene.' This sense of newness is emphasized by his declaration that 'it was a night for new friends'; even the nightfall outside the club as he parts ways with a potential new lover is likened to 'a needle on a new song...descending.'

Our second poem is Taylor Johnson's 'Club 2718.' Consider here how, unlike in Keene's poem, the physical club is not accessible to the speaker and thus its dance floor is 'a room that exists occasionally inside of [them]'. The speaker's intentions are clearly and quickly stated in the line 'I was on a gin fueled hunt for big asses and music I could cry to'. Notice how the poem moves away from the parameters of the club, how we find ourselves in an intimate (though heated) moment with the speaker and their 'woman'; with the speaker's grandmother and grandfather; in other 'rooms' within the speaker where music plays and video memories are looped. There is a paralleling of the speaker's own romantic relationship and its back and forth nature ('I wept in the winter / when I left my woman, I wept in the heat when she came back') with that of the speaker's grandparents (a grandfather who the speaker sometimes believed 'owned [their] grandmother kept her overfed and out of the sun in the back room' but also remembers him 'dancing a limber legged shuffle and singing across the wall to [their] grandmother'). Here, the external-made-internal, or completely metaphorical club is a site of desire, of hunger, of thirst, "of knowing, not knowing" that extends into the speaker's memory, into their love life.

Lastly, let's look at Danez Smith's 'The 17-Year-Old & the Gay Bar'. In this poem, the underaged speaker is 'blessed' with entry into a gay bar, a 'gin-heavy heaven'. As with Keene and Johnson, the speaker tells us what's brought them here: the 'need to be needed, to belong'. The speaker is free – the energy of this night, these men so precious, it is likened to the divine. On the dance floor, they fashion a deity of their own from a beautiful stranger with whom they share a dance and a kiss. Notice, as with Keene, a moment of transformation in the last line, the speaker's self-realization cutting through their own frenzied praise: 'or maybe I'm just tipsy and free for the first time, willing to worship anything I can taste'. What the speaker has risked for this night earns them an unprecedented sanctuary, a 'blessed ground to think *gay* & mean *we*'.

Now that we have some examples to work with, it is your turn to reflect on a memorable night out (or multiple!). Take five minutes to write down every sensory detail you can remember: what you wore, what you ate/drank, who you went with. What did the venue look like? "Dimly lit" like the dance floor of Club 2718? How did the music sound? How did the people look?

Once you have a sizable list of concrete details, begin to consider your place in the bar/club/lounge/venue. How did you feel? Did you feel like an outsider or like you were among friends? How did the sounds/imagery of the event affect you? Were you impressed, enthralled, disgusted, alarmed? Overstimulated, bored? What did you come looking to find? Was it there? What did you realize, learn? What or who did you gain? What or who did you lose?

You're free to stop here and decide if you have enough material to begin crafting a poem. You could also take it a step further as we see in Johnson's poem and begin making associative leaps away from the nightlife experience(s) and toward other aspects of your life, history, and/or memory. Be whimsical, free, and open with these leaps – you never know where you'll end up.

Once you're satisfied with your free-write, construct the first draft of a poem that evokes your experience. Let the language be as glamorous and shimmering or as grimy and dank as the night itself. Think: if this bar/club/lounge could talk, what would it sound like?

Finally, remember to have fun with it. As we galivant into the night reaching for joy's hand in the first place, so let it guide your writing and revision process.

Follow the poem as it leads you. It will be quite the dance partner.

Further Reading
John Keene, *Playland* (Seven Kitchens Press 2016).
You can also find links to the poems by Danez Smith and Taylor Johnson mentioned in this article at <https://linktr.ee/poetrywales>.

SL GRANGE

Erce, Erce, Erce, eorþan modor

Yan

And George Hill is a golf course now diggers
downed and common storehouse yielded up with
hedge enclosed and bunkered all the final
waste of grass gone rotten in the August
sun we flee in airplanes bound for other
uncommoned places hot with monument
and travelsick with histories of loss
from this overview try to hawkeye some
manor of truth in the dusty patchwork
watching a small fly batter itself out
stupid against the small window the light
whilst for a moment in a green field down
there a fox hangs in mid air as she leaps
the brook and above her the rook calls

Tan

A blackbird sings the evening to itself
flies over fences into the blue and
double-glazed we channel switch I read that
charity begins at home yet so do
walls and doors and locks now a small boat rocks
on the rising waters borders closing
fast on those without and those within so
cry nostalgia for hedgerows if you like
true there are rare birds who rely on them
to survive but these thin margins draw us
dragged backwards through forests long rubbed out lost
made meagre the ghost beaten boundaries
made spectral the hare hunched fox-frighted in
her form and the bodies buried beneath

Tether

I heard William the Conqueror lay
in state too long swelled and burst exploding
putrid viscera over the gathered
robber barons who left him there to stink
packed their saddlebags with land and rode back
into the plundered forests claiming blood
lines and nobility and property
whilst in the wild woods stags stand watching still
prick antlers into mists and mellow is
not the word for this September's swelling
just ask William whose belly full of
venison could not stop rooks from leaving
unwanted omens in a hunted land
hare all red sinews splayed in a green field

Mether

Monarchs and men made haunch rump and cutlet
of common wealth ruled straight lines across us
bound us to maps and weighed us down with sacks
full of bent pennies crown and shilling lost
deep in mud in mire in empire laid to
rest for some and hard labour for others
some hedgerows are a hempen line snapping
straight rare birds that did not survive this
the way the past like a rainbow's end moves
away from you as you try to step to
wards it the way the present is a gift
and an unbearable performance
the way the future is a fireball
that you do not look up in time to see

Pit

By the time your easy jet has spun out
a Surrey spiral above Heathrow or
the ferry carried you from Dover to
Calais or the tide flowed indifferent
over Morecambe Bay you have died of a
surfeit of light on water and the slow
rust of everything except a system
made of lies you realise kings and queens
are like the rest of us they shit swell and
burst when dead I woke up to a man's voice
disembodied telling me we were bought
together by his definition of
grief to which I reply if that's what you
see happening you really aren't looking

Aayther

From high rise windows London is forest
roots grow through both geography and time
this tongue is a temporal migrant a drift
the land speaks ancient dialects worn hard
with underuse and wretched nationhood
Erce hung from a rotten tree swings to
the carrion call and the wormery
of fucked earth all tidied-up hills naked
rape seeded cling film wrapped with ownership
mouth wide beneath the plastic bag of lords
land hoards old dragons whip-tailing their cash
smoking out the vermin as if their blood
is not the same as if their guts are stuffed
with sugar true that and tobacco too

Sezar

Smoke cigars on George Hill play another
round the fox has run off has gone to ground
the plane descends the queen is dead is death
we delved and dug and in the hole we made
we placed a coin a rainbow and a flame
a knotweed curse sugar retribution
an uncanny unheeded unhedging
Eve spins alone there are no gentle men
so cast the hex eorþan modor take
our tithes in mulch and tilth and teeth and fur
we re-member each other we lick our
selves clean of all this history all this
rotten flesh throw our strange seeds to the air
to forest famished fields to rooks to hare

Overa

I dreamt a house at night and outside was
a chicken wire fence and through an open wind
oh leapt a taxidermy fox her grin
all ragged as she looked at me glass eyed
her sawdust spilling on the kitchen floor
she said the doors are locked you got it wrong
mistook the outside for the inside
the woods are   waiting not
for you   but just because
that's   what woods   do   the weeds
         will eat the   walls
away   in time in   time
         they   will   eat
you
         too

ZOË BRIGLEY Introduces a Compendium of Very Short Poems

From the haiku to the cinquain, the best writers of short poems make the writing of them look easy. The short poem needs substance; it needs to contain questions and surprises, to be strong enough to stand rereading, but to offer itself cleanly. We could turn, like Bitite Vinklers, to epigrammatic folk poems and songs, or to aged proverbs or ancient languages in Ankit Raj Ojha, James B. Nicola, and Jean Atkin. Some poets lean into the intensity of a moment as Aidan Semmens and Ilias Tsagas do here. Others examine what is provoked by the external world: the sycamore seeds in Heather Mackay Young's and in Jack Houston's poems speaking very differently about marriage or perseverance. There are realizations for the narrators of Alison Whittenberg and Carrie Etter in contemplating lost mothers, or there are surprises in terms of imagery in Alix Edwards and Camille Francois. When you are an editor reading thousands of poems on a regular basis, it is hard to be surprised, but all of these poems did just that – they surprised me!

I Do Not Weep
Translated by BITITE VINKLERS from a Latvian Folk Poem

I do not weep
For the dead,
I do not wear out my eyes;
The dead will not rise—
I need my eyes for living.

JAMES B. NICOLA

puddle

The puddle sat and stayed day after day night after night
The puddle growing old collected dust dirt grease and oil
The puddle in the moonlight glistened some said beautifully

ANKIT RAJ OJHA

Span

जईसे जईसे दुबवा जामे ओईसे ओईसे दंतवा जामे
(May my teeth grow like grass.)
– Bhojpuri proverb, sung by kids while sowing their baby-teeth in soil

Long after greed gnaws
last leaf of the earth,
fangs will outlive corpses
where nothing else grows.

JEAN ATKIN

Listening in Icelandic

þ
thorn is sharper, distinct at its tip
holds a raindrop pricked onto each
sound that cannot be extended while

ð
eth whispers like its own ghost
trailing a cloud behind it as if you
brushed by softly through the reeds

AIDAN SEMMENS

Stairwaddy

soft wind
tapping
at the window

the skirl
of the night-
calling curlew

ILIAS TSAGAS

Moraba Albaloo: Persian Sour Cherry Jam

After Ramita Navai's *City of Lies: Love, Sex, Death and the Search for Truth in Tehran*

Two construction workers are sitting cross-
legged on a torn cloth laid out on the elevated
part of the pavement, under a canopy of trees,
eating bread and homemade cherry jam: sweet,
sour and red as fresh blood.

ALLISON WHITTENBERG

Lag

When you realize,
Please return the library books
They're on the table
As her last words
Balances every *I love you* she'd given

Instead of goodbye
The incessant, familiarity of instruction
   the sum
                  of my mother

CARRIE ETTER

The Wedding

As I sweep into the Bath registry office on no one's arm, I survey the room to see so
many friends, former students, my fiancé's relatives, and at the front, standing, smiling,
Trevor, in a suit with a burgundy tie to match my Biba dress. As I make my way to the
centre aisle, I notice a single empty seat. There my mother is and isn't, and I pause,
acknowledge her presence and absence as I take a step, then another, toward joy.

HEATHER MACKAY YOUNG

Contemplating 'Failed Marriage'

Winged seeds fall
from the sycamore tree

twirl until they touch a place
they belong—

JACK HOUSTON

every attempt

each year the sycamore
on the bottom corner of the estate
opposite the Co-op
coats the road & paving stones
with countless once-swirled seeds

ALIX EDWARDS

Definitions

I am a woman wronged, sheltered
under blazing red hair. I carry
shame like a string bag of groceries.

CAMILLE FRANCOIS

Labia

Not as a cat's tongue, but an eyelid
Half-closed in weariness, yet
Lucid.
Who says nothing to those who know
No language other than their own.
Unnamed for so long, imagery
Is offence.
All it wants – a stare.

POETRY WALES

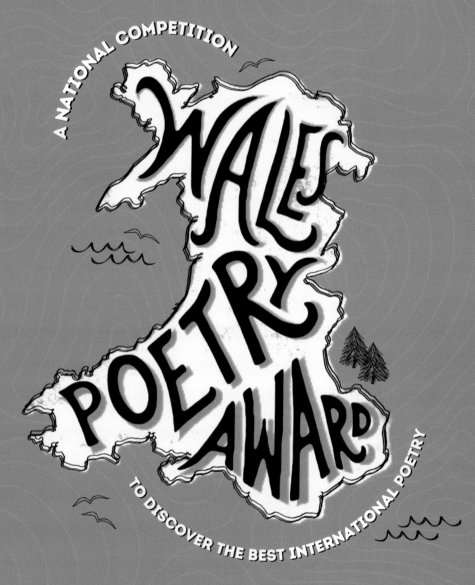

A NATIONAL COMPETITION

WALES POETRY AWARD

TO DISCOVER THE BEST INTERNATIONAL POETRY

POETRY WALES' FLAGSHIP SINGLE-POEM COMPETITION RETURNS!
JUDGED BY DENISE SAUL | OPEN NOW, CLOSES 05.02.24
1ST PRIZE £500 & RESIDENTIAL COURSE AT TŶ NEWYDD WRITING CENTRE

WWW.POETRYWALES.CO.UK/WALESPOETRYAWARD2023

POETRY WALES

WALES POETS YOUNG AWARD

Calling all young poets! Flex your creativity by entering *Poetry Wales'* Wales Young Poets Award!
Write a poem on the theme of Peace in English or Welsh
Entrants must be aged 10-17 and live in the UK
Enter between 10th July - 31st December
For more information including resources for writers and teachers, visit www.poetrywales.co.uk

Yn galw ar bob bardd ifanc! Hyblygwch eich creadigrwydd trwy fynd i mewn Gwobr Beirdd Ifanc Cymru Poetry Wales!
Ysgrifennwch gerdd ar thema Heddwch yn Gymraeg neu Saesneg
Rhaid i ymgeiswyr fod rhwng 10 a 17 oed ac yn byw yn y DU
Gallwch gofrestru rhwng 10fed Gorffennaf a 31ain Rhagfyr
Am ragor o wybodaeth, gan gynnwys adnoddau i awduron ac athrawon, ewch i www.poetrywales.co.uk

IFANC GWOBR CYMRU BEIRDD

Wales Poetry Award Winners

FIRST PRIZE

KATHRYN BEVIS

Translations of Grief

Denial
We meet each week. I tell her who I am
today: how, in disbelief, I am a nursery
of sardines. *Go on*, she says, and I speak
of our flicking, cross-hatched skins, our silver,
shoaling bodies, the swallowtail of our fins.
I explain our obedience to the pull
of colder currents, how we dine on blooms
of plankton, how oblivious we are as dolphins
wait to herd us toward a surface snatch,
as gannets mass to fire themselves — gold
hooded — a thousand arrows to the sea.

Anger
Next time, I'm fury sitting there. Zipped
in a zebra suit, my nostrils flare. One word
from her and my body is a bucking bronco
that never wants to stop. I'm fabulous,
of course — a fashion model with a perfect
arse — dressed to kill in symmetrically
shredded tights. I launch the designer
handbag of myself, thrash my tail and mane.
I hoof the box of tissues, boot old Freud
and Jung and Klein onto the floor. My kick,
we find, is fierce: too much for me to bear.

Bargaining
Friday, midday again, and I'm here
on the dot as a lyrebird on her chair.
I shrill, she nods in time to the rhythm
of my tiny, clockwork heart. I'm haggling
today with chirrups, whistles: *What if?*,
If only..., Why? Rehearsed on the forest's
velvet-curtained stage, I negotiate
with all I've got these days: the tune
of chainsaws, the song of car alarms,
the camera shutters I must mime. I open
my throat, descant my own demise.

Winning Poems 2023

Judged by Gwyneth Lewis

Llenyddiaeth
Cymru
Literature
Wales

Winning Poems 2023

Judged by Gwyneth Lewis

Llenyddiaeth
Cymru
Literature
Wales

Depression
At last, one day, I come as myself.
The quiet holds us both. I try
to tell about the blue whale I'm trapped
inside. There's so much we don't yet know
about blue whales: how many they are,
and where they go to breed. But she knows
as well as me that a blue whale's heart
is the size of a Ford Fiesta: each chamber wide
enough for a drowning woman to pummel
herself against, each beat a boom against
her bones, a deep-sea detonation.

Acceptance
The months strobe by. I shapeshift again,
   again, begin to believe
in the transubstantiation of the flesh.
I am a deep-sea jellyfish, pulsing
disco lights of green and yellow, red. I am
a black-capped squirrel monkey leaning
on a ledge, an elephant doggy paddling
in the rain. I feel my fins grow in. I know
this darting synchrony: I am sardines again.
I am the white ibis who stands one-legged on a rock.
To the sound of distant thunder, I am
the bushbuck — alive, *alive* and licking salt.

SECOND PRIZE

STEPHANIE GREEN

Clara the Rhinoceros

Inspired by the Indian rhinoceros toured by Douwemont Van der Meer throughout
Europe in the 18th century and the painting *La Mostra del Rinoceronte* by Pietro detto
Longhi, 1751 – (Ca'Rezzonico, Venice).

Orphaned pet, two-months old,
squeaking and squealing at the Nabob's table,
a tiny black horn sprouting
on top of your nose, a unicorn in armour:

Saucer-slurper, short-sighted snuffler,
licker of titbits from ladies' fingers
sucking with your delicate prehensile lips.
So adorable – your eyelashes and ear-fringes.

But once an adolescent, you lost your charm.
You'd outgrown yourself, dragging
your own warty skin like a tramp
wearing all her coats at once.

Bath-time was lily-pond Armageddon.
Your swivelling bulk too big for drawing-rooms,
porcelain-smasher, clock-toppler:
a cacophony of percussive smithereens,

zithery shivers and xylophone crescendos
of glass and marble drum-rolls,
and your pant-squeak, honk-bleat, roar-shriek,
ears and tail erect in shock.

Fortune-maker, wild card, the joker in the pack.
So your Grand Tour of Europe began:
gentle giant, three-toed ungulate,
Clara the Rhinoceros and her Potent Horn.

A sensation!

Bouffant wigs àla rhinocéros all the rage.
Beer-quaffing and pip-spitting your delight.
Oh, the joy of oranges at Versailles!

Now here, in the capital of exotics, Venezia,
Carnival revellers crave the new:
bulge-eyed ostriches, neck-gyrating giraffes,
and you, the ultimate Rococo grotesque.

Jaded pleasure-seekers, Venetians know
that below the grandeur of the Palazzo Ducale
lie dungeons of sighs. They too
want to shiver at the whiff of the damned.

But you, inscrutable as an idol, wreathed
in tobacco smoke, ignore the crowds:
Bautas, muzzles raised like wolves,
and the black Morettas, mirrors to your dark.

You turn your back on them, refuse to budge,
only a skin-twitch to whip-flicks.
Your verdict a turban-like turd of splendour
and stench, laced with orange-sweet urine.

Winning Poems 2023
Judged by Gwyneth Lewis

Llenyddiaeth
Cymru
Literature
Wales

THIRD PRIZE

KIT GRIFFITHS

Marshfield

I found the toadstools under our bed
enchanting – Mum said, "Try not to breathe too deep?"

I found her passed out on the new living room floor - I darted
for the phone, dialled nine-nine- she sprang up like Uma Thurman
"Very good, BUT you should've checked my mouth
for chewing gum, in case I choked."

Before we'd finished unpacking, I snuck on the 007 cd – we
drop-rolled doorway to doorway, clutching loaded bananas.

This was the summer we ran

in and out, squealing, bed-trampolining,
flinging and fainting off sofa arms,
strutting, once, down the dinner table
in imaginary cowboy boots
to 'A Change Would Do You Good.'

This was the summer we listened
to our quiet in place of silence.

My brother raised sunflowers higher than the house.
At least, above the bungalow's gutter –
his flowers loomed higher in the hot blue sky
than the man we were in hiding from.

Llenyddiaeth
Cymru
Literature
Wales

Winning Poems 2023
Judged by Gwyneth Lewis

WALES POETRY AWARD

DUOS: VIRGIL SUÁREZ & JO MAZELIS

ZOË BRIGLEY introduces two poems about butchers

What a duo we have for this issue: one poem set in Havana, Cuba, the other in Swansea, Wales, but both have interesting things to say about the butchers depicted and their handling of meat. Virgil Suárez's poem is much closer to the butcher, the narrator's father, and the commentary on his butchering of horses for the local zoo is also a commentary on family, survival, and how as children, we observe adults who dominate and sustain our lives. Jo Mazelis's narrator is more distant, admiring the skill of the butcher, though like Suarez, Mazelis is travelling back in time, here to 1963. Regardless, both poets use a shorter line effectively to unfold each butcher's significance.

VIRGIL SUÁREZ

Horsemeat Vernal Equinox

My father butchered horses
to feed the tigers and lions
at the Havana Zoo. I saw
his cuticles pinked by residue
At night the dry air popped
my nasal capillaries, *cabezitas
de vena*, my mother called
them. The trickle of constant
blood flowed down my throat.
A cotton ball stopped the blood
from staining my pajamas
or pillow. When the flow stopped,
I pulled the cotton slow
and a tendril of coagulated
blood oozed from my nose
and I kept it on the nightstand.
In the morning the dried up curlicue
of blood looked dark and crispy
like what I imagined horse entrails
looked like. Horses with ticks
gorging in their ears. Mosquitos
and flies tormenting my father
and the other butchers. Yes,
we ate horse meat which my
mother made into *tasajo*
and served over *boniato blanco*.
We ate what my father brought
home. At sunset we watched
the sky blush with yellow orange.
The cigar smoke wafted
in the humid air. The frogs

jumped on the cool porch tiles.
Green spots by the windows.
The crickets and fireflies buzzed
in the grass. Sometimes the only
place to be is right where you feel
the weight of sleep taking you
down. A river darkening in light.

JO MAZELIS

Bacon Stall, Swansea Market, 1963

I see his hands, meaty as ham hocks
and the precise line of his determined mouth,
the faint bristle on his mid-morning chin.
The knife is long and slim,
sharpened on a steel
with a musical scraping sound.
The meat, held captive under the press
of his hand's pink heel, has a dry
crust of white fat over seashell flesh.
He draws his blade down and across
in one slow move.
Rashers fall like petals onto the scarred
wooden board.
No one told me that history was written there
in his hand-carved bacon's poetry.

REVIEWS

Vanessa Lampert
Say It With Me
(Seren, 2023, £9.99)

Rosie Jackson
Love Leans over the Table
(Two Rivers Press, 2023, £10.99)

Helen Mort
The Illustrated Woman
(Chatto and Windus, 2023, £12.99)

It's a rare delight to be able to review three such dazzling collections, each in their own way revolving around observation, vision, and the potency of the act of looking.

Several poems within Lampert's keen-eyed, warm-hearted, and original debut collection, *Say It With Me*, turn the poem into a time-travelling vessel, a Tardis, a way to retrieve those who have become lost along the way. In 'When You Are King,' the speaker endows her dead brother with the glory of footballer Gordon Banks:

> ... you loved
> that man with a small boy's clean love –
> ... Only the living crown the dead
> so I'm making your life like Gordon's
> I'm making you squint under a bright
> sun.

The line endings here tell their own story, particularly "loved" and "love", moving as they do between the past and present tense as a form of wish fulfilment. The present tense of the title, 'When You Are King', works in the same way, childlike in its belief that it can reimagine the past in order to change it, devastating in the power that it has to do so only functions within the realm of the poem.

In the collection's first poem, 'Not Like

This Park', and throughout, Lampert uses the power of negation to offer us alternate visions and versions of reality. In the speaker's park, there are: "No crouching spikes of glass in grass, ... no *Fuck off* gouged on a bench/ ... No bags of shit dangling from branches/like baubles." Instead, we are given a park which is: "... a bowl to hold sunlight/ ... no one in my park but us. The warm weight/of your hand in my hand." The poem is alive with sensation, particularly the visual and tactile. Inside it – despite its conjuring ills by naming them – we know we are safe, given permission to choose our own world, and fill it with beauty. From Lampert, we learn again how large the sphere of the poem can be, how it can hold side-by-side a sense of both beauty and fragility.

In 'Josser's We' (josser is a circus term for an outsider), having painted the circus folk themselves as: "...self-assured, lithe, / justifying summer with their thighs. / ... shining like a shoal of jubilant fish", the poem's speaker cries: "If this is a dream then hide the truth/from me. There are so many lovely things/that we can't hold or keep." Again, the willingness, the wilfulness of the vision is offered to us as a gift. Although we know the illusion (and know the poem's speaker knows it, too), we are permitted into a restorative world of "neon painted spandex"-clad folk "pirouetting, irresistible to doves," a world inside which we can choose to dwell for as long as we like.

There is belief at work here, not a religious faith – in 'What the Horses Told Us' she writes "I'm pretty sure I've never had God" – but belief nonetheless in the imagination's power to offer us alternative visions for our lives. "I'm changing what happened" writes Lampert in 'Wimbledon 2020'. The charm of the trick is that, over and over again throughout this collection, we believe in and become emotionally and intellectually invested in Lampert's lovingly reimagined lives.

In the central section of *Love Leans over the Table*, 'Better Than Angels,' Rosie Jackson's poems, by contrast, are faith based by nature. In the act of writing about mystics', anchorites', and other spiritual and religious figures' visions or 'shewings,' she sets in motion two spheres – the seen and the unseen; light and dark; wordlessness and language; silence and sound; dynamis and stasis – in an effort to create a dialectic between them. In 'St Bede: From Winter to Winter', her speaker avows: "I brush the arms/of implausible beings, angels moving/slowly moving between snow and shadow." The verb choices here, "brush", "moving", and again "moving", depict a state halfway between stasis and movement. The feeling here is dreamlike, as though we are being invited to swim through a honeyed chasm between mortality and immortality: "...*caught/in this blue land between dust and light*." Similarly, the images of "snow and shadow" whirl between a half-state between darkness and light. I'm reminded of Vincentio's monologue in Measure for Measure (Act III, scene i) where the Duke meditates on mortality:

Thou hast nor youth nor age,
But, as it were, an after-dinner's sleep,
Dreaming on both.

Jackson's collection is replete with allusions to other texts yet is still brim-full with fresh-minted images. "Listen", her speaker of 'St Bede: From Winter to Winter' cautions, "...if you would hear the gods breathe, /you must be stranded from yourself."

This vision of self-alienation as a condition for intimacy with the divine plays out in many of Jackson's poems. In 'The Recluse Tells of her Love', an affecting monologue in the voice of an Anglo-Saxon anchorite, (usually a woman who has retired to a solitary place, often to a single cell built at the side of a church, to lead a life of seclusion and spiritual meditation.) Here, the speaker proclaims her vision for life eternal:

Here I am untrusset from all wordly
    woes.
Here I am undeadlich. I am the spus of
    the Lord.
...Unhope have I none ... Godd hisself
    is with me, his brethe swote,
smellinge of lavender and mire.

This is a poem that impresses immediately, not only with its deft use of Old English but also in its use of negation. Rather as Lampert's poems offer us alternative visions and possibilities for our lives, Jackson's use of 'un' words, "untrusset... undeadliche ... unhope," speak of a renunciation which makes alternate realities possible: a Christian release from the world's unhappiness in "untrusset" (unbound), a deliverance from mortality in "undeadlich" (eternally alive) and a release from despair in "unhope." Without these negations, the recluse would not be able to make the sublimely audacious statement, shimmering with certainty, "Godd hisself is with me," nor claim for herself the spousal intimacy with him that would allow her to experience his "brethe swote" (sweet breath). The depth of Jackson's painstaking research, her eyes-wide-open image making, her facility with other vocabularies, her allusions to other texts, and her fellow feeling for the mystic tradition make this collection a rare and magnificent thing.

Far from simply characterizing a God without fault, in 'The Anchorite's Mother' (another monologue) we hear the poem's speaker grappling aloud with the problem of pain, the puzzle of a world created by an all loving, all powerful God, yet one in which we inhabit in suffering: "What upside-down creator would take such trouble/to make life, if he wanted it cast away? She thinks/of a sprig of willow trampled, heel by heel." The speaker's anguish at her daughter's embrace of a life of isolation within thick walls, inside an almost windowless cell, in a vastly shrunken world without society, touch or colour, has deeply uncomfortable echoes of Genesis 3:15. Here, as the narrative has it, God punishes Satan for tempting Eve and Adam to eat the fruit that was forbidden to them by putting: "enmity between you and the woman, and between your offspring and hers; he will crush your head, and you will strike his heel." Later in this section of *Love Leans over the Table*, in 'There Will Be No Epigraph,' an unnamed anchorite declares everything she has lost by responding to her vocation, her vision. She declares:

> I died to skin. I died to my babies
> unborn
> ... I died to colour.
> Oh, I died to colour, as if He has no
> patience
> with turquoise and madder.

By contrast, Helen Mort's latest collection, *The Illustrated Woman*, is full of skin, of colour, of inking the skin and of the sexual politics inherent to the act of looking at a woman's tattooed skin. In 'First Tattoo by a Woman,' Mort writes:

> Holly, colouring me for days in Crookes
> to the tune of Action Bronson,
> my pale hip rising to the needle, blood
> rising
> to flower under her touch ... Then,
> afternoon
> and the scalpel gaze of a stranger on the
> beach,
> his kids in the shallows and him
> transfixed

In disparity to the oddly pleasurable tactile, auditory and, crucially, the consensual experience of being carefully tattooed by a female artist, "to the tune of...", "blood rising/to flower under her touch", and the intimacy of the proper names here, "Holly", "Crookes", and "Action Bronson", we are shown the purely visual, non-consensual "scalpel gaze" of an unknown, male stranger. Mort's speaker is left vulnerable, wanting to put "something bright/between me and his curiosity."

The poet gives us a sense of her own power and agency when she writes from the perspective of the female gaze. In 'Tollaidh' she writes of: "... how much I wanted you to turn around, /wanted the landscape of your body / ... the track winding away from us, / the off-gold light. The sight of it." Relatively unused as we are to reading poetry by a woman who is clear about her sexual desires, brings surprise and delight. The revelation or epiphany in Mort's final line, a vision she and her lover share equally, "out towards Slioch", is underscored by the closing cadence of the marriage of full rhyme on "light" and "sight". We finish this collection with no illusions about our need to embrace new feminisms and feminists.

In the poem 'Deepfake: a pornographic ekphrastic' the stakes couldn't be higher in terms of male violence, image manipulation, lack of consent and revenge pornography. At the back of the collection Mort writes about her own painful experience of someone who had taken "... non-intimate images of me from social media sites and manipulated them to create violent porn, accompanied by threatening descriptions." Within the poem she writes:

> This is you doing your worst.
> This is language reduced to words.
> This is me using you hard in a poem
> where I decide what's shown
> *I want to see her humiliated. Whore*
> I am not humiliated. I am heavy
> bored ...

The playful near-rhyming couplets

"words ...worst", "poem... shown",
"*Whore* ... bored", are tauntingly musical,
indeed musicality is a strength shown
throughout the collection and one of its
great pleasures for its reader. Mort's
triumphant tone here, her conscious
snatching and shifting of agency within the
poem must meet with a resounding and
unified response from her readers,
including me: *Amen.*

KATHRYN BEVIS

dir. Keith Wilhelm Kopp
Translations
(Kopp Productions, 2023)

Translations, a new feature length
film from director Keith Kopp in
collaboration with screenwriter
Laurence Guy, is a rumination on trauma,
isolation, mental health, and the act of love
– both the love of another and the love of
oneself – with a poet at its centre. The film
has already made several waves within the
cinematic world, as a multiple award-
winner at the Riverside Film Festival 2023,
bagging the Audience Choice Award for
Best Feature Film, Best Actress, and Best
Screenplay. This is something of a new
medium to review in the pages of Poetry
Wales, being a fictional film about poetry,
the poet and the active role of poetry in
our lives.

Films about poets often position
themselves around famous poets; if one
were to think of 'poetry films', we might
think of Matthew Rhys or Tom Hollander's
interpretations of Dylan Thomas, or
Cynthia Nixon as Emily Dickinson. For
these films' merits, they reside in the realm
of the historical and edge (to a lesser or
greater degree) in on the sometimes-
dangerous area of fictionalising or even
trivialising the lives of real people. Where
Translations finds its success as a 'poetry
film' is in its central character, Stef, played
by Kate Morgan-Jones.

In starting with a fictional, present-day
poet, *Translations* sets itself apart
immediately as a film shouldering the
contemporary act of writing poetry. The
film is extraordinarily present; filmed
during the early lifting of restrictions at the
tail end of the 'bulk' of the Covid-19
pandemic, it marks itself as a living piece
of art concerned with the world as it is
now. Stef is an agoraphobic translator and
poet, who receives a houseguest in the
form of her deceased brother's friend,
photographer Evan.

The film is not about the COVID-19

pandemic but stirs a resting memory of life in lockdown as Stef and Evan share both a living space and a trauma in their grief for Stef's brother's passing. As Stef completes a translation of old letters, Evan adjusts to her agoraphobia, eventually persuading her to read some of her poetry for him.

During a screening of *Translations* at Chapter Arts Centre, Cardiff, I had the pleasure of discussing the production of the film with the director, screenwriter, and lead actor, and was somewhat shocked to discover that Laurence Guy is not a regular writer of poetry. The verses he prepared for the film are immediate and contemporary and you could easily be mistaken for believing Guy was a poet-turned-screenwriter, rather than vice versa. Of the poems Stef shares, a clear comparison can be made between her work and the performance poetry advanced by organisations like Apples and Snakes and Button Poetry. It is lively, rhythmic, and made for the stage. Although they are English language poems, they carry more than a little *cynghanedd* beat, emphasising the bilingualism the film wears on its spine:

Walls
flat-packed
double-wrapped
jutting
confusion
a momentary illusion
walls that divide and keep us inside
while
others do shelter
protect us from all

The success of the poems in the film measures well against the story at its heart, and in its emphasis of the importance of featuring a poet as a lead character in the drama. It considers poetry as an act of communication with an overwhelming outside world, and the script follows Stef's initial reluctance to share her words with the world through an act of betrayal and ultimately acceptance. Her poems carry her through her trauma and out into the world, leading her to new opportunities. There is a delightful re-framing of her first poetry reading of the film when it reaches its conclusion, though you will have to catch a screening of the film to fully enjoy it.

Ultimately, the film carries moral ambiguities in its depiction of Stef's poetry being 'leaked' to success – but this makes for a more interesting journey towards the conclusion. It is refreshing too, to see a poet depicted with a day job that she is also passionate about – far too often, poets are depicted (or even considered in real life) to be waiting for the success of mainstream acceptance in what it would not be unfair to say is a niche art form. The realism of this appealed to me and the production team behind the film must be congratulated for this.

Kate Morgan-Jones and Alan Emrys must also be celebrated for their portrayals of people coping with shared grief in very different ways; it is their relationship which summons the poetry to a public space, and the performances from both actors play a large part in conveying this.

The world of cinema can be argued to be somewhat convergent with the world of literature and especially poetry when it comes to the general audience member or reader, with a certain amount of emphasis placed on trends in the market that are then driven to work until cultural fatigue sets in. Translations is a reminder of why independent cinema is important, in its defiance of this, acting to not only put poetry at the centre of its story of isolation and trauma, but also in its promotion of bilingualism. It shows us boundaries, then urges the audience to cross them, cross back over, and welcome a release from isolation.

GEORGE SANDIFER SMITH

Christopher Reid
Toys / Tricks / Traps
(Faber, 2023, £13.99)

Philip Gross
The Thirteenth Angel
(Bloodaxe Books, 2022, £12.00)

Glyn Edwards
In Orbit
(Seren, 2023, £9.99)

The art of poetry is a subjective affair – and beauty is in the eye of the beholder. But it was a pleasure to review these three books – *Toys / Tricks / Traps* by Christopher Reid, *The Thirteenth Angel* by Philip Gross, and *In Orbit* by Glyn Edwards – all of which exuded quality and craftmanship. Whilst their approach and styles differ, the underlying theme of being human really shines through – Reid taking a memoire-style approach of his childhood, Gross with an earthly human narrative and Edwards with a driving emotional force. In an age of nihilism and social fracture such work is an important and grounding place to remember our shared humanity.

The opening poem 'The Hero' from Reid's collection *Toys / Tricks / Traps* recalls fond, yet distant, memories of childhood:

Snapshots remember those far days for
    me:
days when the camera doted on me
and could not keep its eye off the little
    hero.

The words set the scene for a personal journey through youth that is both melancholic and wistful. Remembering days gone by – inner snapshots capturing infancy, childhood, and adolescence.

It is a personal memoire of a young Reid – captured through the worldly filter of a mature mind casting his eye back over life. That is what makes this book more special –

the presence of both versions of the self (the younger and older) inextricably tied despite the passing years. The opening poem ends with the older Reid observing his younger self from a distance, yet opening a mental space that connects the two:

A present with a future in it –
seventy years of future, and counting –
hidden from the questing infant hero
ever more deeply as time goes by.

The atmosphere builds throughout the book. It is a careful selection that allows the prisms of joy from one's childhood to flash through. One cannot help but be transported to one's own childhood in the process. The simple beauty of 'I Spy', our collective childhood game, to the nostalgia of 'Wonders', about a family holiday.

The poems are nuanced and layered. 'Fog' recollects another snapshot – this time a photograph of figures in fog – "smudges of off-black", "God-like" in the freeze:

Fixed there, the figures, for all that,
    are not lost.
This is the element in which they live;
    where I lived, too.

In those lines, we get a sense of what the poet is looking to achieve – to create in aspic moments that are not lost, but alive. The journey from childhood to one's latter years can be painful through the filter of retrospect; but what matters is what we take with us and the living connection between our present, past, and future selves. In 'The House Itself', Reid passes what we assume was his childhood home, seen "on the rare nights I visit now". The poem is cast in a scene of "perpetual twilight, a morbid sepia gleam" – of broken walls and shaky fences – and ends with the barbed observation: "but at least I am reassured it is still alive". The image disturbs but we understand the truth of those passing years.

At times, we get a sense of a very English upbringing. A Home Counties world of a young Reid "larking about" with talks of "pluck and making do". We visit a world of boarding schools, dormitories, and a Latin teacher with a "pipesmoked moustache" ('Silly Owls') and a boy "swoony with hormones" ('Lucretius, He Say'). 'Prospectus' encapsulates this particularly English world. Such poems felt more daguerreotype than kodak – but this added to the otherworldliness of the journey.

One is left feeling that this was Reid's attempt at reconnecting with his inner child. In 'Little Self', he begins: "Little self, I'd like to know you better". In his gentle plea, Reid ends with a lament to bridge the gap: "The one adult who would have been happy to join you in conversation is simply too far away". For the outsider, Reid did make the journey. And we hope he does so again.

Philip Gross's collection *The Thirteenth Angel* starts at the most natural place: 'Nocturne – The Information'. The scene begins at night, which is typical of the theme of this book – darkness. In fact, it is not until the last few pages of the collection than any light is allowed to enter. The opening piece is a sprawling, uncompromising burst through city life.

It is clear, as one journeys with Gross, that the title of the book is misleading. The collection has little to do with any ephemeral divinity (or indeed Godly angels). It is very much an earth-bound book weighted by the elements and gravity of a mortal life. We are reminded of the living elements of Earth – that Gross re-conjures in what feels, at times, like a deliberate reality-check. The collection brims with reminders of who (and what) we are and the hard, collective journey we have made (and make) on the planet – from the geological shifting of continents and lava flows to the day-to-day grind of modern life and the pandemic. In 'Porcelain' he says:

I don't know
what kind of perfect crockery
Pangaea was, the mono-continent,
before God's whim
to send it splintering.

The poem 'Paul Klee – the Later Angels', however, encapsulates the poet's approach to this book. For Gross, the spiritual is here in the material world:

Some of his finest, final angels
are not bodies at all.
Not 'spirit'. They are the intersections of
        the things –
shapes, colour-bodies, masses –
that make up the world.

Or in the poem 'Ash Plaint in the Key of O', Gross talks of the "higher mathematics" when describing the multiplying leaves of the Ash tree. This is a mind rooted in the reality of the material world, celebrating, and mourning it for all its beautiful flaws.

But there is a sense of contradiction in the book. Instead of fully embracing the raw bleakness of the 'Divine-less' existence, Gross references the spiritual and religious innumerable times – with mention of Psalms, monks, angels, even Lucifer. Given the driving, earthly force of the collection, one naturally wonders why the frequent reference to the spiritual. This adds to the sense of a past spiritual life – perhaps discarded in the brutality of one's own journey. For all the power of the words, these shadows are difficult to hide. And yet, each time Gross introduces us to religious concepts, he quickly shuts the door. In 'A Q'ran of Ruzbihan' (about the 16th century Islamic ornamental and decorative Holy book), Gross focuses on the calligrapher, colourist and patternmaker and emphasises (rightly) their artistic contribution to its creation – yet not the spiritual aspect accounting for their presence in making their holy book.

Or in 'The Mishnah of the Moment' (Mishnah referring to the Jewish oral tradition) – there is further suggestion of the scars of a discarded spiritual enquiry. And in the last poem 'Silence Like Rain', Gross references the 'sangha' (the community of Buddhist monks) – where again, the poet sees only the grounding reality of the material plain. One is left feeling that Gross doesn't quite escape the 'shadows of paradise' – and there is a sense of anguish and pain that emerges: "How could God sleep between creating days but in His darknesses?".

This is a collection that challenges the reader. It tackles big subjects with a force of its own. A sobering experience that frustrates and delights in equal measure – and ultimately leaves us wanting more.

Glyn Edwards' *In Orbit* begins with 'elegy' – a lament of loss:

before beginning
please understand
there's no end here
in dark is dark
in night is night
in grief is grief

A blunt, singular blow of a poem that punches through the page with the intention to daze, which it does. It is an apt opening for a collection exploring the full face of bereavement. Edwards constructs an entire universe centred around a first-person narrative of grief, mourning the passing of a beloved teacher, a raw exploration of emotional damage. The poet takes us on a roller-coaster ride exploring human frailty, loss, and the impact such events have on our lives – and the screeching halt that enters our world when someone close to us suddenly dies.

The second poem 'she rang to say you'd collapsed' is the marker for the rest of the collection. It describes the moment of death which casts its long shadow over the book, becoming the point where all the pieces are thrown into flux – cast into

orbit and left drifting in its shattering aftermath.

The poem 'the bells in their gables were stilled' is a sobering piece about the funeral and reverberates with pathos. It begins with the words "the stars on the ceiling were subdued, sad." And then "I've seldom seen the hall so filled, began the vicar and the congregation turned as a single corvid mass." But the poem ends with a primal, near-savage line of the person looking into the coffin: "Nothing would have reassured you in death for your face had slipped sideways from its skull and the left eye was whiter and wider, and your left cheek had lurched, and the nostrils were taut and your lips were lost in palsy."

But the stand-out piece is "if one day you woke up and the Eiffel Tower was gone". It plays on our familiarity with the imposing image of the Eiffel Tower, but invites 'personification' as we imagine a loved one in its place – asking how we would feel if it suddenly disappeared:

it's because it's gone – the iron that
        shaped the sky, the light,
the spell – all gone, in no time at all,
        days, hours even, the city
would begin the tiny acts of erasure all
        grievers do:
understanding the dark; taking detours;
        forgetting.

The book ends with the poem 'dark matter' that draws together the shattered world of loss. It ends with the line "this empty space is all that is left of you" – and the reader is left trying to comprehend their own emotions and the seriousness of life. Ourselves now cast into a fractured orbit of our own.

With those stark words ringing in our ears, we turn to the 'Afterword' at the end of the book and are told that the "characters of *In Orbit* are fictional constructs". We are left trying to process our triggered emotions and trauma whilst coming to terms with the fact that this was actually a work of fiction. This feels jarring, but in some way maybe it helps. We were given the opportunity to explore and relate to real-time loss – and then brought back from the edge of grief.

This is a powerful book and a strong collection. Edwards creates a world in which the pain of loss and bereavement can be fully explored. An analytical psychologist would approve of this Jungian approach in using the imagination for trauma therapy – not to ignore it but to sit with our pain (whether bereavement, guilt, sadness, or trauma) and to release it through understanding and self-healing.

These collections reminded me of the importance of writing – writing for therapy, writing to remember, and writing for the sheer pleasure of creating new worlds on the page. Or new ways of healing parts of our shadow-self. Jung was the master of analytical psychology – and showed us the way to clear damaged and repressed aspects of ourselves by facing our demons head-on through careful introspection. Poetry (particularly well-crafted poetry such as here) can be a powerful vehicle that allows us to really sit with our pain and fears – and to sooth and heal ourselves through poetic alchemy. As Gross suggests, God may have sent Pangaea (and us) splintering, but these poets have shown the human way to heal – like a poetic form of *Kintsugi*. We should all take a leaf out of Reid's book and go visit our little selves once in a while – for our own sake and theirs.

GWION IQBAL MALIK

Abdulkareem Abdulkareem (he/him) Frontier III, is a Nigerian writer and linguist. His works appear and are forthcoming on National Museum of Language, *POETRY Magazine, Transition Magazine, SAND Journal, MIZNA, LOLWE, Qwerty Magazine* & elsewhere. He reads for *Agbowó Magazine* and *Frontier Poetry.*

Jean Atkin's latest publications are *Fan-peckled* (Fair Acre Press) and *The Bicycles of Ice and Salt* (Indigo Dreams). Her third full collection *High Nowhere* is forthcoming in 2023 (Indigo Dreams). Her work appears in *Pennine Platform, Raceme, Anthropocene, Finished Creatures, One Hand Clapping* and *Acumen.*

Cary Archard is the founder of Seren Books, and the editor of *Welsh Retrospective*, a selection of Dannie Abse's poetry, and *Dannie Abse: A Sourcebook.*

Thea Ayres is a poet from West Yorkshire. She is a graduate of the Writing Squad. Her work has been published in *The Scribe, Ink Sweat & Tears, Strix* and the *North*, and has been commissioned by Dead [Women] Poets Society and the Arc Project.

Kathryn Bevis's pamphlet, *Flamingo* (Seren, 2022), was one of the Poetry Society's 'Books of the Year' and her poem 'My body tells me that she's filing for divorce' was shortlisted for the Forward Prize for Best Single Poem – Written – 2023. Her debut collection, *The Butterfly House*, is forthcoming (Seren, 2024).

Jane Burn is a working-class, autistic, pansexual hybrid writer. She is widely published. Jane has an MA in Writing Poetry. In 2022, Jane explored her neurodivergent writer's experiences, funded by ACE. In 2023 she received a grant from the RLF. Her latest collection, *Be Feared*, is available from Nine Arches.

Chaucer Cameron is the author of *In an Ideal World I'd Not Be Murdered* (Against the Grain 2021) which is part memoir/part fiction and explores the impact of prostitution. Chaucer was short listed for Live Canon 2021. She is co-editor of the online magazine, *Poetry Film Live.*

Sophia Rubina Charalambous is a Cypriot-Kashmiri journalist, writer, director, and poet, born and raised in London. Her poetry appears in *Popshot Quarterly, Bad Lilies, Magma, Mslexia, Finished Creatures,* and *Ink Sweat & Tears.* Shortlisted for the Alpine Fellowship Poetry Prize 2022, Sophia is working on her first pamphlet.

Claire Crowther has published five collections. The first, *Stretch of Closures*, was shortlisted for the Aldeburgh Best First Collection Prize and the fourth, *Solar Cruise* was a Poetry Book Society Recommendation. She teaches poetry at Oxford University and is Deputy Editor of *Long Poem Magazine.*

Tony Curtis wrote the book on Dannie Abse for the Writers of Wales series. He gave the 2007 British Academy Walton Lecture on Dannie's "Persistent Irony and Reluctant Faith". Dannie was in the audience. His eleventh collection, *Leaving the Hills*, will be published by Seren next April.

Jose Hernandez Diaz is a 2017 NEA Poetry Fellow. He is the author of a chapbook of prose poems: *The Fire Eater* (Texas Review Press, 2020) and the forthcoming, *Bad Mexican, Bad American* (Acre Books, 2024).

Australian **Cath Drake's** collection, *The Shaking City* (Seren), highly commended in the 2020 UK Forward Prize and longlisted in the Laurel Prize, followed *Sleeping with Rivers*, a Poetry Book Society choice & winner of the *Mslexia* pamphlet prize. She hosts The Verandah, poetry teaching & events. https://cathdrake.com

Saddiq Dzukogi is a Nigerian poet and Asst. professor of English at Mississippi State University. He is the author of *Your Crib, My Qibla* (University of Nebraska Press, 2021), winner of the 2021 Derek Walcott Prize for Poetry, and the 2022 Julie Suk Award.

Alix Edwards's art tells stories about women, many of whom society has dismissed or ignored. Alix is a Cynefin creative, lead artist for Treorchy Time Capsule and Representing Wales 2022-23 writer. Her poems have appeared in *Haus-Arrest, Penny Thoughts* and *Marble Magazine.*

Carrie Etter's fifth collection, *Grief's Alphabet*, will be published by Seren Books. She is a member of the creative writing faculty at the University of Bristol.

Camille Francois holds a PhD in contemporary British literature and has taught at Cambridge and several French Universities. She now lives near Paris and teaches at an international secondary school. Her poems have appeared or are forthcoming in *The North, Wild Court, Anthropocene, Magma,* and *Under the Radar.*

Karen Goodwin was born in Swansea in 1976. She received an Eric Gregory Award and her poems have featured in Seren anthologies and magazines including *Stand, Poetry Wales,* and *The Rialto.* She is Poetry Editor of *Sabotage Reviews.*

S.L. Grange is a poet and theatre maker. Winner of the 2021 Poetry Wales pamphlet competition, SL Grange's recent work includes the series 'Letters of No Moment', for the National Archives, and Difficult Matter, a residency and exhibition at Parlour Gallery, Deptford

Stephanie Green's pamphlets are *Glass Works* (2005), shortlisted for the Callum McDonald Award, *Flout* (HappenStance, 2015) and *Ortelius' Sea-Monsters* (Wigtown, 2023) winner of the Alastair Reid prize. Poetry/sound walk, *Berlin Umbrella*, appeared in Berlin in 2018, StAnza 2020 and Rewilding in Orkney 2023.

Kit Griffiths is a 34-year-old, Cardiff-born and raised (Merthyr on weekends), Cambridge-educated and Margate-based poet. Kit has just been selected for the Southbank Centre's New Poets Collective 2024.

Philip Gross's *The Thirteenth Angel* (Bloodaxe, 2022) was shortlisted for the TS Eliot Prize. He is a keen collaborator, e.g., with artist Valerie Coffin Price on *A Fold in The River* (2015), with Lesley Saunders on *A Part of the Main* (2018) and Welsh-language poet Cyril Jones on *Troeon/Turnings* (2021)

Richard Gwyn is a poet and novelist, author of *The Vagabond's Breakfast*, which won Wales Book of the Year for non-fiction in 2012. He is also a translator from Spanish, notably of *The Other Tiger: Recent Poetry from Latin America.* Richard is Professor in Creative Writing at Cardiff University.

Bethany Handley (she/ her) is a writer and disability activist living in Pontypridd. Her poetry has been published in *POETRY, Spelt* and on the Poetry Foundation and the Institute of Welsh Affairs. Bethany's work typically explores ableism, inaccessibility, and her relationship with nature as a Disabled woman.

Lydia Harris has made her home in the Orkney island of Westray. In 2017 she held a Scottish Book Trust New Writer's Award. Her first full collection, *Objects for Private Devotion* is due from Pindrop Press this summer. Westray Writers meets in her lounge, looking over the Atlantic and North Sea.

Paul Henry was born in Aberystwyth and came to poetry through songwriting. His collections include *Boy Running, The Glass Aisle* and *As If To Sing* which won this year's *Wales Book of the Year* Poetry Award. His selected poems, *The Brittle Sea*, was recently reprinted by Seren. www.paulhenrypoet.co.uk

Lynne Hjelmgaard, originally from NYC, divides her time between London and Aberystwyth. Her books include *Manhattan Sonnets, The Ring, A Boat Called Annalise, A Second Whisper* and *The Turpentine Tree*, her latest collection with Seren (Oct. 2023).

Jack Houston is a parent, writer, and public-library worker. Their work has appeared in *The Butcher's Dog, Finished Creatures, The London Magazine, Magma, Poetry London, The Rialto* and *Stand*, among others. A debut pamphlet, *The Fabulanarchist Luxury Uprising*, is published by The Emma Press.

Christodoulos Makris's most recent projects are *Contemporaneous Brand Strategy Document* (Veer Books, 2023) and *It Reeks of Radio* (BLR Editions / UCD, 2023). A former Writer in Residence at Maynooth University, he received a Literature Project Award from Arts Council of Ireland. He is the poetry editor at gorse journal.

CONTRIBUTORS

Gwion Iqbal Malik is the Poet in Residence at the Dylan Thomas Birthplace in Swansea. He works as a Probation Officer and is also editor of Frequency House. His collection *Enter The Ziggurat* was released in 2021. His spoken-word album *Religion of Moonlight* is available on Bandcamp.

Jo Mazelis is the author of three acclaimed short story collections, including the Commonwealth Best First Book Shortlisted *Diving Girls* and the Welsh Book of the Year shortlisted *Ritual, 1969*. Her novel *Significance* won the Jerwood Prize. She is currently working towards her first poetry collection.

Fabio Morábito was born in Egypt to an Italian family. When he was fifteen, his family relocated from Milan to Mexico City, and he has written all his work in Spanish ever since. He has published five books of poetry, five short-story collections, one book of essays, and two novels, and has translated into Spanish the work of many great Italian poets of the twentieth century, including Eugenio Montale and Patrizia Cavalli. Morábito has been awarded numerous prizes, most recently the Xavier Villaurrutia Prize, Mexico's highest literary award, for *Home Reading Service* (Other Press, 2021). He lives in Mexico City. The poems translated here appear in *A cada cual su cielo* (Visor, 2021).

A poet and editor from North Carolina, **Tangie Mitchell** (she/her) is an Obsidian Foundation alum and has received support from the Cave Canem Foundation, the Center for Black Literature at Medgar Evers College, and Sundress Academy for the Arts. She holds an MFA in Writing from Sarah Lawrence College and lives in Harlem, New York.

James B. Nicola's seven full-length poetry collections include *Fires of Heaven* and *Turns & Twists* (2021-2022). His poetry and prose have received a Dana Literary Award, two *Willow Review* awards, one Best of Net, one Rhysling, and ten Pushcart nominations. His nonfiction book *Playing the Audience* won a *Choice* award.

Gboyega Odubanjo was born and raised in East London. Gboyega published two pamphlets: *While I Yet Live* (Bad Betty Press 2019) and *Aunty Uncle Poems* (winner of the New Poets Prize from the Poetry Business 2021). We are sorry to add that Gboyega died suddenly at the end of August 2023. He was 27 years old.

Ankit Raj Ojha is a poet and assistant professor of English from Chapra, India. He has a PhD from IIT Roorkee. He edits *The Hooghly Review* and is published in JHUP, Routledge, Sahitya Akademi, *Outlook, Stanchion, Dreich* etc. He is the author of *Pinpricks* (Hawakal '22). Website: https://linktr.ee/rajankit

Nurain Ọládèjì is a Nigerian writer. His work has appeared in *Transition, Acumen, Olongo Africa, Dunes Review, The Chaffin Journal*, and elsewhere. He lives in Lagos, Nigeria.

Ben Rhys Palmer was born in Cardiff. He won 1st prize in the Verve Poetry Competition in 2022. His work has been commended in The Winchester Poetry Prize, The Interpreter's House Poetry Competition, and the Welshpool Competition. His poetry has appeared in *The London Magazine* and *Forklift, Ohio*.

Stephanie Powell is a poet based in Naarm / Melbourne. Her latest collection of poems is *Gentle Creatures* (Vagabond Press, 2023). atticpoet.com

Sheenagh Pugh is Welsh and lived in Cardiff for many years, but now lives in Shetland. She has published many collections with Seren, plus a novel and a critical study on fan fiction. She has also published a novel with the Shetland Times Publishing Company, *Kirstie's Witnesses*, which was recently reprinted.

Billy Ramsell was awarded the Ireland Chair of Poetry Bursary in 2013 and the Poetry Ireland Residency Bursary for 2015. His second collection, *The Architect's Dream of Winter*, was shortlisted for the 2014 Irish Times / Poetry Now award. He lives in Cork where he co-runs an educational publishing company.

Born in Llandudno and resident in London, **Jeremy Robson's** most recent collections are *The Heartless Traffic* and *Chagall's Moon* (both Smokestack Books). Formerly the *Tribune* poetry critic and CEO of Robson Books, he edited *The Young British Poets* (Chatto), and with Dannie Abse, a series of critical anthologies for Corgi Books.

Jacqueline Saphra's is the author of nine plays, five chapbooks and five poetry collections. Her second collection, *All My Mad Mothers* (Nine Arches Press) was shortlisted for the TS Eliot Prize and her fifth, *Velvel's Violin*, a Poetry Book Society Recommendation, was out from from Nine Arches Press in July 2023.

Joshua Seigal comes from Welsh Jewish ancestry. He is best known as a children's author and was the recipient of the 2022 People's Book Prize. He has several collections of poetry published by Bloomsbury and is an Official Ambassador for National Poetry Day. Joshua's online home is www.joshuaseigal.co.uk

Aidan Semmens's first collection, *A Stone Dog*, was published by Shearsman Books in 2011, thirty-three years after his first pamphlet. There have been five more volumes, most recently *The Jazz Age*, a sequence of surreal vignettes chosen by Salt Publishing to relaunch Salt Modern Poets in October 2022.

Owen Sheers is a poet, author, and playwright. Twice-winner of Welsh Book of the Year he was recipient of the 2018 Wilfred Owen Poetry Award. A former NYPL Cullman Fellow, he is *Cennad* of WalesPENCymru, Professor in Creativity at Swansea University and co-founder of Black Mountains College, a new college focused on systems change and sustainable futures.

Penelope Shuttle lives in Falmouth. Her next publication will be a pamphlet titled *Noah*, from Broken Sleep Books in December 2023.

Paul Stephenson has three pamphlets: *Those People* (Smith/Doorstop, 2015), *The Days that Followed Paris* (HappenStance, 2016), written after the November 2015 terrorist attacks; and *Selfie with Waterlilies* (Paper Swans Press, 2017). He helps curate Poetry in Aldeburgh. His debut collection is *Hard* (Carcanet 2023).

Virgil Suárez was born in Havana, Cuba in 1962. At the age of twelve he arrived in the United States. He received an MFA from Louisiana State University in 1987. He is the author of eight collections of poetry, most recently *90 MILES: SELECTED AND NEW*, published by the University of Pittsburgh Press.

Ilias Tsagas is a Greek poet writing in English and in Greek. His poems have appeared in journals like: *Apogee, Ambit, Sand, FU Review, Plumwood Mountain* and elsewhere. He has also published poems in anthologies like: *Deviance* by Toothgrinder Press and *Disease* by Carnaval Press.

Richard Maggraf Turley won the 2007 Keats-Shelley Prize for Poetry and is author of the collection *Wan-Hu's Flying Chair* (Salt, 2009), which won the 2013 Wales Book of the Year 'People's Choice' award. He teaches in the Department of English and Creative Writing at Aberystwyth University.

Bitite Vinklers, a translator of Latvian literature, has work in anthologies in the USA and UK and such journals as *The Paris Review* and *Kenyon Review*.

A three-time Pushcart Prize nominee, **Allison Whittenberg** is an award-winning writer and teacher for the Indiana Writers Center. Her novels are *Sweet Thang, Hollywood and Maine, Life is Fine, Tutored* (Random House 2006, 2008, 2009, 2010). She has a short story collection, *Carnival of Reality* (Loyola UP 2022).

Heather Mackay Young is a poet, healer, and graduate of The Glasgow School of Art. Her writing has been published by *Poet Lore, Hummingbird Press*, and *Olney Magazine*. She is the 2023 Anne-Marie Oomen Literary Fellow at Poetry Forge. Heather lives and writes on the Isle of Lewis in Scotland.

Jane Zwart teaches at Calvin University, where she also co-directs the Calvin Center for Faith & Writing. Her poems have appeared in *Poetry, Threepenny Review, The Poetry Review, Ploughshares*, and *The Moth*, as well as other journals and magazines.